Explosion of Evangelism

D. James Kennedy's
Explosion of Evangelism
*The Evangelism Explosion ministry:
past, present, and future*

Thomas H. Stebbins, D.D.

EVANGELISM EXPLOSION
PUBLISHING
FORT LAUDERDALE

PUBLISHED BY
EVANGELISM EXPLOSION INTERNATIONAL
PUBLISHING
FORT LAUDERDALE, FLORIDA

Copyright ©2002 by Evangelism Explosion International. All rights reserved. No portion of this book may be reproduced, stored in a retrieval system, or transmitted in any form or by any means—electronic, mechanical, photocopy, recording, or any other—except for brief quotations in printed reviews, without the prior permission of the publisher.

Unless otherwise indicated, Scripture quotations used in this book are from the Holy Bible King James Version.

Anecdotes in this volume are based on fact; however in some instances, details have been changed to protect identities.

Book Design by Mike Ferraguti and Jill Noonan

Printed in the United States of America.

*In honor of the great multitude of
volunteers who truly make this ministry
flourish and who add joy unspeakable
to the journey.*

OTHER BOOKS BY TOM STEBBINS

Evangelism by the Book
Missions by the Book
Truyen Giao theo Thanh Kinh
(Missions by the Book in Vietnamese)
Friendship Evangelism by the Book

Contents

Letter of Congratulation viii

Special Appreciation ix

Foreword by Rev. Kennedy Smartt xi

Introduction xvi

Chapter 1: God Makes Some Changes in Jim Kennedy 1

Chapter 2: Evangelism Explosion Goes Worldwide 19

Chapter 3: North America: Evangelism Begins at Home 35

Chapter 4: The Gospel Is for Everyone 53

Chapter 5: Europe: EE's Most Daunting Continent 73

Chapter 6: Wide, Wide Is Oceania 89

Chapter 7: Asia: The Populous Continent 105

Chapter 8: Africa: The Hungry Continent 121

Chapter 9: Latin America: The Explosion Has Been Dramatic . . .139

Chapter 10: Eurasia: A New Day of Opportunity 155

Chapter 11: The Decade Ahead 173

Appendix: Back through the Years in Photos 189

Letter of Congratulation

February 2002

Dear Jim and Anne,

Heartiest congratulations on Evangelism Explosion International's completion of forty abundantly fruitful years of ministry! You have truly impacted the world for Christ!

As a director serving on EE's International Board and a regular supporter of the ministry, I am delighted to see the EE ministry has grown and been blessed beyond anyone's expectation and is the first Christian ministry to be planted in all 212 nations and 15 territories of the world.

All praise to God for the millions of Christians trained to share their faith effectively and the tens of millions of lost sheep who have been brought to Christ's fold!

Helen and I pray God's blessing upon you, the EE staff and all those who are involved in this exciting ministry on every continent.

Yours in Christ's abundant harvest!

"Love ya,"

Rich

Rich DeVos

Special Appreciation

THIS BOOK IS the synergistic product of many EE leaders, associates and friends. To all of them I'm deeply grateful. I want to thank especially . . .

- Dr. D. James Kennedy for granting me the freedom to write this book. He and his lovely wife, Anne, have contributed immensely to its inspiration and production.

- My beloved wife, Donna, for supporting me in prayer and encouragement during the long hours and late nights I spent at my laptop.

- Beverly Wallhoff, my executive assistant, for her patient and excellent help in typing, proofing, photocopying and caring for a multitude of other support tasks.

- Rev. H. Robert Cowles, editor *par excellence*. He has an outstanding ability to make narrative and dull detail exciting.

- Dr. Herbert Lee Williams, author of *D. James Kennedy, The Man and His Ministry*, for his willingness to allow me to quote freely from his excellent book.

- Richard M. DeVos, EE Board Member, for his gracious letter of congratulation and generous gift that made the printing of this book possible.

- William G. Runde and his friendly staff at Commercial

Printers for such a quality printing job and for his generous gift toward the printing of this book.

- Rev. John Sorensen, my beloved son in the faith and EE Vice President for Ministry Advancement, for suggesting this book and assisting with its production.

- Mike Ferraguti, EE Director for Creative Services; and Jill Noonan, Graphic Artist, for their beautiful design and layout of the book's cover.

- Each of our EE vice Presidents, Regional Directors and National Directors for supplying valuable historical and statistical data so essential to this book.

- Bobb Biehl, President, Masterplanning Group International, my life-long friend, mentor, and consultant, for his valuable suggestions regarding the book and its cover.

- Gladys Israels, James Carlson, Ruth Rohm, Mary Anne Bunker, Anne McDonough and Shirley Engebretsen, who supplied vital historical information from EE's beginnings.

- *Operation World* for valuable geographic and statistical information referred to in the chapters dealing with EE's ministry overseas.

Thomas H. Stebbins, D.D.
March, 2002

Foreword

by Rev. Kennedy Smartt

JIM KENNEDY ARRIVED at Columbia Seminary in Decatur, Georgia, in the fall of 1956. At the time, I was pastoring Ingleside Presbyterian Church just three miles from the campus. I was a recent seminary grad myself, one of several who had a special passion for evangelism. Bill Iverson, who figures in Chapter 1, was another.

Bill Iverson had been my fraternity brother in college. Even then, we had done some evangelizing together. After we both were out of seminary and in pastorates, I invited Bill, in 1959, to come to Ingleside Church for evangelistic services. We visited homes all day and sometimes late into the night. Bill would take one layman and I another. We both saw a significant number of people come to Christ. Sometimes Bill would get to the church just in time to preach. I would be a nervous wreck, but if he was talking to someone ready to receive Christ, he would forget all about time.

The next year, as we at Ingleside Church were planning evangelistic services, I remembered Jim Kennedy. He and Anne had often attended our church, if Jim wasn't out preaching somewhere. Jim and I shared a mutual concern for evangelism, and our people at Ingleside (and I) were challenged by Jim's conversion testimony. Not only that, but Jim had led a young

Explosion of Evangelism

Swedish classmate at the seminary, Willy, to faith in Christ. Willy's testimony swept the seminary and Ingleside Church, where he began attending after his conversion.

So in 1960, a year after Jim had finished seminary, I invited him to come for ten days of evangelistic services. I couldn't think of anyone who would be as willing as I believed he would be to visit all day long and then preach in the evening.

When we went out calling the first Monday morning of the crusade, none of the people on my list was home. But as we drove down one of the streets, I saw Mr. Robinson sitting on his front porch, a man whom I had recently visited in the hospital. We stopped, and Mr. Robinson invited us in. From our questions, we discovered he was not trusting Christ for his salvation, so we shared the Gospel with him. Though he was very interested, he held back from making a decision. He said he wanted his wife to be in it, and she was at work. He asked us to come back the next morning, when she would be home.

We left Mr. Robinson on cordial terms and returned to our car. But I was impressed by the Holy Spirit that we should not leave without Mr. Robinson's making a decision So we went back in. This time Mr. Robinson did receive Christ as his Savior. He promised that he and his wife would be at church that night, but later called to say that his wife could not make it. They both would plan to be at the crusade Tuesday night.

Tuesday morning Mr. Robinson died of a heart attack. Jim and I went to his home and led the bereaved wife to Christ. She asked if I would conduct her husband's funeral.

"Please tell the congregation that he was saved the day before he died," she said, "because otherwise no one will ever believe he has gone to Heaven!"

We were in a community where everyone knew everyone else, and the story of this man's conversion spread like wildfire.

Foreword by Kennedy Smartt

A large congregation gathered for his funeral and I was able to spot many in the group who were not Christians. I made plans for Jim and me to visit them in their homes. For the rest of that week, and on into the next, whenever anyone hesitated to receive Christ, we would answer, "Remember Mr. Robinson." Over and over again we found people ready to give their hearts to Christ. I am convinced that God, in His providence, arranged all those events just so Jim Kennedy could get a vision for what would, in time, become Evangelism Explosion.

You will read in Chapter 1 how a radio preacher and a newsstand book brought about Jim's conversion. It is obvious to me, and it will be to you, as you read this book, that God had a very special plan for a very special person. By God's enabling, Jim has accomplished one of the most remarkable feats in all the history of the Church. His evangelism strategy and training have literally penetrated every nation and territory in the world!

I don't mean to suggest that Jim Kennedy is some sort of superman. Like each of us who are Christians, he is a sinner saved by grace. But Jim Kennedy is different from most us because He had a vision and believed that His God was great enough to make it happen.

Jim Kennedy, since the day he had this great vision, has never wavered or faltered in its pursuit. Even without Evangelism Explosion, Jim is one of the busiest and most productive men I have ever known. But if you know him as I have been privileged to know him, you know that the foremost passion of his life is evangelism.

All of us can praise God for that!

Rev. Kennedy Smartt, D.D.
Retired

Introduction

A FEW YEARS after my missionary career in Vietnam ended with the fall of South Vietnam, I found myself in Hong Kong. I was ministering to an English-speaking congregation of some 60 people. For a year I preached my heart out. Not one convert. Still 60 people. Nothing was working. I was totally discouraged.

In the providence of God, a missionary with OMS International, "Buddy" Gaines, had a recommendation and a book. The recommendation was Evangelism Explosion, and the book (you guessed it!) was *Evangelism Explosion!*

To my great surprise, it worked! It worked because Evangelism Explosion (or EE, as we have come to call it) is biblical, spiritual, and transcultural.

Buddy Gaines helped me launch Evangelism Explosion in Kowloon Tong Alliance Church. During our first "semester," 40 people professed faith in Christ, and 35 of them became a part of our congregation. We did it a second time with similar results.

By then, other English-speaking pastors in Hong Kong were asking to be trained. When they carried EE back to their churches, they discovered that EE worked for them, too, and our congregation at Kowloon Tong grew to 360!

Before EE, fear gripped me whenever there was opportunity to share the Gospel one-on-one. I preached on the importance of equipping saints for ministry, but I was clueless as to how. I knew God wanted Christians and churches to win others, but it seemed like an unattainable ideal.

EE has changed all that!

This book is the story of why and how EE has worked for hundreds of thousands of other pastors, missionaries, and lay people in North America and everywhere else on the other continents and in every nation and territory of the world.

It can work for you, too!

> Thomas H. Stebbins, D.D.
> Executive Vice President
> Evangelism Explosion International

 # Dr. D. James Kennedy
Founder and President

"Together we can change the world"
- Dr. Kennedy to his congregation in 1962

Chapter 1

God Makes Some Changes in Jim Kennedy

SUPPOSE, BACK IN the 1950s (if you were around then), God had asked you to find someone to lead a worldwide evangelism explosion. You could be excused for not considering Jim Kennedy.

Jim was born November 3, 1930, during his parents' two-week stopover in Augusta, Georgia, on a trip from Jacksonville, Florida to Chicago. He was the second son of a traveling salesman and an alcoholic mother. George Kennedy, Jim's father, was regularly on the road, industriously seeking markets throughout Illinois and as far south as Georgia and Florida. Of Irish extraction, George and Ermine Kennedy were nominal Methodists; in practice, they had no spiritual roots.

"If the Gospel had anything to say about my situation," Jim reflects, "I never got the message."

Yet from age six, young Jim sensed that God had something for him to do. He thought about it often on his walks to and from school in Chicago "It was a feeling," he says, "that I could not explain."

Explosion of Evangelism

In his early teens, young Kennedy became involved in competitive sports and also joined the Boy Scouts, working his way up to the rank of Star. He became proficient on the clarinet and saxophone. He dreamed of becoming a scientist, preferably an astronomer.

When Jim was 15, the family moved to a suburb on the southern fringe of Tampa, Florida. Across the city, in North Tampa, another transplanted youth, Billy Graham, was beginning his studies at Florida Bible Institute (now Trinity College). But neither knew the other in those days.

By his senior year, Jim's proficiency on the clarinet made him top performer at Henry B. Plant High School. At the annual band concert Jim prepared himself well for his solo in Gershwin's "Rhapsody in Blue." He was unaware that the University of Tampa's music director was in the audience. His flawless execution of the solo won him a full scholarship at the university!

Jim was soon playing first-chair clarinet at the university. As he pursued his degree, he also became involved in other extracurricular activities: rowing, judo, weight lifting, ping pong, dancing, boxing. He liked both music and dancing. When the local Arthur Murray studio placed an ad in the newspaper, Jim, on impulse, responded.

He was hired on the spot as an instructor. "At 25," Jim says, "I was a bona fide swinger!"

Happier on the dance floor than he ever had been during his years at the university, he became expert enough to take first place in Arthur Murray's all-American competition. Predictably, Jim Kennedy moved up the salary scale until be became studio manager of the Tampa franchise.

Still, Jim had no room in his life for church, for God, for the Bible. Worse, his selection of friends steered him into a godless

God Makes Some Changes in Jim Kennedy

lifestyle. "Occasionally I drank. My language was corrupt. I did a little carousing. All in the name of a good time." Jim looks back on those years with regret and a sense of shame.

A New Applicant Arrives

One breezy Friday evening, Anne Lewis walked into Jim's dance studio. She wanted to sign up for lessons. For the young manager, it was the proverbial love at first sight! "She was beautiful," Jim remembers yet. "Petite in size, blue eyes, long dark wavy hair that broke over her shoulders, a captivating smile." Until that moment, he had hardly given a thought to marriage. But that, too, was about to change!

"I told a fellow instructor, 'That's the girl I'm going to marry!'"

Anne Lewis was born in North Carolina, but her veterinarian father soon moved the family to picturesque Lakeland, Florida, just 34 miles from Tampa. Both parents were active in the local Presbyterian Church. Dr. Kenneth R. Lewis was an elder and Anne's mother was president of the women's ministry and pastor's aide.

Anne herself was heavily involved in the same church, singing in the choir, soloing from time to time, working with children. But about one thing she was emphatic: she never wanted to be married to a preacher! "Life in a goldfish bowl is not for me," she insisted.

Not so surprising, Jim found Anne Lewis to be the most promising dancer he had ever held in his arms. Immediately he signed her up for ten hours of instruction, then for six more months of instruction. Studio rules forbade dating between instructors and their students. But as soon as the course of lessons was finished Jim invited Anne to a picnic with the other teachers and their friends.

Anne held down a secretarial job by day. But she was also a busy performer in water-ski shows as a water ballerina. And on the weekends, she dated Jim, riding the train between Lakeland and Tampa. "I feel like a commuter!" she said in one of her letters to Jim.

Rather early in their three-and-a-half-year courtship, Anne had a question for Jim.

"Where do you go to church?" she asked.

"Nowhere," Jim replied. And then, to defend his negligence, "You don't have to go to church to be a Christian. You can be just as good a Christian without going to church."

Almost in a whisper, Anne replied, "No you can't!" Jim was not prepared for her soft-spoken but firm answer.

"I was utterly taken aback," Jim Kennedy remembers. "I had never been challenged like that before. I was amazed that anyone would have the audacity to say such a thing."

One Sunday afternoon—sleeping in rather late—with Anne's gentle assertion still echoing in the remote recesses of his mind, Jim was aroused from a deep sleep by his clock radio. Presbyterian pastor and radio evangelist Donald Grey Barnhouse was on the air.

"He was the last thing I needed in my bedroom," Jim says. "I got up to tune in some good music. But before I reached the radio, this Presbyterian minister stopped me dead with a question that practically set me back on the edge of my bed.

"In that stentorian voice for which he was famous, Dr. Barnhouse asked: 'Suppose you were to die today and stand before God and He asked you, "What right do you have to enter my heaven?"—what would you say?'"

In that electrifying moment Jim Kennedy felt totally disarmed. He groped desperately for the answer he did not have.

God Makes Some Changes in Jim Kennedy

The Change Begins

The crucial, dynamic change in Jim Kennedy's life began to take place as he listened intently as Dr. Barnhouse explained God's plan of redemption. He was hearing the Gospel for the first time, praying, confessing his guilt and his need. Suddenly he became curious about the Bible, even though he hadn't the slightest idea where in it to start looking. Above all, he was filled with a strange and wonderful awareness that he had passed from death to life.

There was another influence as well. He visited the corner newsstand and asked the proprietor if he had any religious books.

"Just one," the man said, and handed Jim a copy of *The Greatest Story Ever Told* by Fulton Ousler. Jim paid for the purchase and took the book to his apartment.

"I went home," Jim says, "and read part of the book every night for the next several days. When I finished the book, it seemed as if the cross of Christ had been erected right in my apartment. Now I knew—for the first time—why Christ was suffering there.

"I slipped out of my chair to my knees and asked Christ to come into my heart. I asked Him to forgive me and cleanse me of my sins. From that day on, my life has never been the same. I shall be forever grateful for the radio broadcast of Donald Barnhouse and the book by Fulton Ousler. God used them both to bring me to a saving knowledge of His Son."

Jim Kennedy's insatiable hunger for spiritual nourishment drove him to a fellowship of believers in a neighborhood Presbyterian Church in Tampa. Right away he was drawn to a Bible class comprised of young people who met on Sunday nights. He began to devour massive chunks of Scripture. Within months, he was asked to teach the class.

Anne noticed the remarkable change in Jim's life. She was delighted to learn he was attending church and teaching a Bible class. As she heard him, over a period of months, retell his testimony again and again, she began to realize that she herself had never come that far. She could see clearly that what she had known was "churchianity," not true Christianity. She wanted the reality she saw in Jim's new faith.

So it happened that the first person God used Jim to lead to Christ was the woman he loved. And Jim began to feel a sense of call growing within him. At first he ignored it. Then he tried to rationalize it away. The dance studio was paying better than ever. Jim's immediate concern was security—self-preservation.

Finally the pressure became unbearable. Late one afternoon, at the end of a busy week, Jim locked himself in his studio office and knelt in desperate prayer. Then he stretched out full-length, face to the floor.

"Lord," he prayed, "do you really want me to quit this job? Are you sure you want to use someone like me?"

Jim had no visions. He heard no voice. But he recalls every detail of the struggle. When he stopped fighting, he got to his feet and picked up the telephone. He could not believe it, but he was calling in his resignation!

But before he could say anything, his boss on the other end of the line informed Jim that he wanted him to take over the Arthur Murray studio in Sarasota as half-owner.

Somehow Jim was able to stammer out, "I'm quitting." When the conversation ended several painful minutes later, Jim found himself without a livelihood. To make matters worse, his once substantial bank balance, which he never bothered to look at, stood at $13.00. No job, no money, no prospect of support!

Jim turned in his keys and left the studio. He went directly to his pastor, who also happened to be chairman of the Presbyterian Home Mission Committee for that area of Florida. Jim's pastor had been impressed by Jim's zeal and teaching ability. He knew of a tiny Presbyterian church located about 20 minutes from Tampa in Clearwater. The church would soon need a pastor.

"Jim," he said, "why don't you go over there and deliver the sermon tomorrow morning at the eleven o'clock service?"

Jim had no reason to decline. Immediately he went to his apartment and began preparing a message. As his text he used Jesus' parable in Matthew 22 about the man who showed up at the king's marriage feast without the required wedding garment. Jim's sermon was a direct outgrowth of his own conversion experience. He could proclaim this text with conviction!

Now that the die was cast, Jim had a proposal to make. It was early December, and the studio gave Jim an unexpected $300 Christmas bonus. That very afternoon, Jim rushed down to a nearby jewelry store, picked out the best half-carat diamond ring he could afford, and headed in his Pontiac for Lakeland.

Later that evening, Jim drove Anne to scenic Lake Hollingsworth, parked the car, reached into his pocket and presented Anne with the ring and this three-part marriage proposal:

1. I have quit my job at the studio, which means I'm almost flat broke.
2. I am going into the ministry, and I know you always said you didn't want to be a preacher's wife.
3. Will you marry me?

The girl of Jim's dreams accepted, sacrificing her personal desires to place her future, and his, in Divine hands. That night—December 3, 1955—became a Kennedy date to remember!

When word got out that Jim was actually giving up his lucrative Arthur Murray career to go into the ministry, some of the folks in Lakeland were shocked. In fact, a few even used the word *fanatic* in describing Jim. But Anne staunchly defended his decision.

Three months later, Anne wrote excitedly to Jim, still in Tampa, saying that she had found the courage to share her Christian testimony for the first time in her life.

"Praise the Lord!" Jim responded. "I prayed that you would have the courage to give your testimony to someone this week . . . Now that you have 'come all the way out for Christ,' you will have power that you never had before . . . I pray that the Lord will let you see some conversions soon. Pray, and you'll have them. Our church deacon raised his hand for salvation. Mrs. Barnum and I prayed for him Monday night. Praise the Lord!"

A Wedding and Ministerial Preparation

Jim Kennedy still needed to resume the long and arduous process of preparation for ministry. Even before quitting the dance studio, he had enrolled that fall in an undergraduate degree program in English. In contrast to his earlier university studies, his A's and B's were not only proof that he had the potential, but testimony of his increasing maturity. Now with his sights set on the ministry, he would need seminary studies as well.

But before seminary, there was the wedding. It took place August 25, 1956, at First Presbyterian Church in Lakeland. The traditional ceremony included Anne's two sisters as bridesmaids and Jim's older brother as best man. The happy couple went off on a Riviera honeymoon—not the French Riviera, but

God Makes Some Changes in Jim Kennedy

Riviera, Florida!

Jim had not yet completed his requisite baccalaureate degree in English. But often a seminary permits an applicant to matriculate with the proviso that the seminary degree is conditional on the completion of the undergraduate studies. In Jim Kennedy's case, he would need to return to the University of Tampa for two additional summers.

Columbia Theological Seminary, seven miles east of downtown Atlanta, seemed like a logical choice. It was a Presbyterian school, and the closest denominational school to Jim's home base of Tampa, where he would need to spend two more summers. Also, Atlanta enjoyed a booming economy, offering excellent job possibilities for Anne. Sure enough, Anne was able to sign on as an executive secretary in one of the city's major brokerage houses. It was a position that enabled the two of them to manage during Jim's three years of intensive graduate study at the seminary.

Three weeks after their wedding, Jim and Anne drove to the campus. They found a garage apartment a half mile from the campus that would be "home" to them for the next three years. "The hardest and happiest of our early life together," Anne comments.

Jim immersed himself in his ministerial studies and excelled academically. He enjoyed the campus fellowship and found time to preach in area churches. He and Anne also availed themselves of some of the city's musical and cultural offerings. The three years passed swiftly. Jim graduated from Columbia cum laude, winning one of four scholarships that he would make use of later.

As the end of seminary approached, Jim gave serious consideration to what lay beyond. He did not feel a specific call to foreign missionary work, but a sermon on the subject convinced him he should at least offer. So he applied to the World Mission Committee as a candidate for what is now Zaire (then Belgium Congo). Anne was totally supportive of her husband, whatever God's will turned out to be.

Two weeks before graduation, Jim had heard nothing from the World Mission Committee. Although by then the most desirable pulpits were spoken for, Jim was advised to send out letters to the stated clerks of five Presbyteries. His letters brought a single response. The Home Mission Committee of the Everglades Presbytery was hoping to organize a new church in the underdeveloped northern sector of Ft. Lauderdale. Jim was welcome to come down and look over the situation.

Jim went. There was not a whole lot to encourage the prospective minister. No building. No budget. No organization. Not even a congregation! A sign on a sandy piece of ground on 50th Street announced to the few pedestrians and motorists venturing out that far from town: "Presbyterian Church to Be Built on This Site." Today 50th Street has been renamed Commercial Boulevard.

In all directions Jim could see only barren space, plenty of weeds, but no people and almost no houses.

"Looks like a good place to begin a church for field mice," Jim commented, not altogether facetiously. "And where does the congregation presently meet?"

"In the small cafetorium of McNab Elementary School just across the town line in Pompano Beach," his host explained.

What to do? There was still no word on his missionary application for Belgium Congo. Meanwhile, Jim was anxious to get to work. Would Ft. Lauderdale be interested in his serving on an interim basis? They would. Jim accepted the schoolhouse church offer on that condition, to begin right after his graduation.

God Makes Some Changes in Jim Kennedy

Church Planters in Ft. Lauderdale

The Kennedys arrived in Ft. Lauderdale early in June. They took two rooms in a motel on Highway A1A, right down on the tourist-crowded beach. In one room they stored their household belongings. In the other they lived. That motel became home to them for the next six months.

The first order of business was to get things ready for the Sunday morning worship service. A small but attractive stage had been built at one end of the cafetorium. Around a veteran piano, Anne began to build a music program. And in that setting the two of them began their Ft. Lauderdale ministry June 21, 1959.

Jim Kennedy waited three more months for the verdict from the World Mission Committee. A disqualifying asthmatic condition had shown up in the course of Jim's physical exam. He would not be going to Central Africa. By the time the report reached them, the Kennedys were totally immersed in their Ft. Lauderdale ministry. They had given missions a serious look. Now it was time to sink their roots in Ft. Lauderdale. The thought of seeking some other place of service never really crossed their minds.

Under the hard work and enthusiastic direction of Jim and Anne Kennedy, the infant church seemed bound to show immediate and rapid growth.

But it didn't.

Attendance, instead of climbing up past the 50-mark, began an unexplainable decline. As the months passed, the decline worsened. The Kennedys worked harder, but the heart-wrenching plunge continued. At the end of ten months, the original attendance of about 45 each Sunday stood at an abysmal 17!

"Extrapolation made it clear," Jim calculated, "that I had

Explosion of Evangelism

two and a half months of ministry left before I was preaching to only my wife—who was threatening to go to the Baptist church down the street!"

Jim knew that something wasn't working the way it was supposed to. Suddenly he put his finger on it. It had to be, of all things, his "invitation" at the end of each sermon to "slip up your hand" or "stand up" or "come forward" to make a public profession of faith in Christ. Worshippers who came from New York, Pennsylvania, Ohio were extremely uncomfortable with this time-tested procedure in the South. If simple invitations couldn't be relied on to build up the numbers, what else? Home visitation certainly was essential, and Jim was pressing it vigorously, yet neither was that approach producing the desired numbers.

Then when Jim was at the very lowest point of his ministry, a letter providentially arrived from a fellow minister whom he had come to know while in Atlanta. Kennedy Smartt wanted Jim to come to his Presbyterian church in Scottdale, Georgia, to conduct a ten-day series of evangelistic services.

"Can you believe that?" Jim asks with amazement. "I, who had just decimated one church was being asked to ship my technique across state lines. 'Have plague—will travel!'"

Nevertheless, Jim Kennedy agreed to go. When he arrived in Scottdale, his host met him with disconcerting news. "In addition to the nightly sermons," the minister announced, "we will be going out every morning, and every afternoon, and sometimes at night after the services. You're going to have an opportunity to witness to these people eyeball-to-eyeball and toenail-to-toenail." He added, "I've saved all the tough ones for you!"

"I was trapped," remembers Jim Kennedy. "I didn't know how to witness to anyone." In his room, he got down on his face before God and prayed for hours. "Lord, You've got to help me!

God Makes Some Changes in Jim Kennedy

I don't know what to do!"

True to his promise, Kennedy Smartt arrived the next morning to take Jim Kennedy witnessing.

The very first encounter had all the makings of a disaster. Then, suddenly, Jim realized what the problem was. "Clearly," Jim declares, "this man was non-elect." But Jim's pastor friend came to a different conclusion: Jim was clearly a non-evangelist. Taking over the conversation, the older minister, in no more than 15 minutes, had the man on his knees receiving Christ into his life. "It was a very traumatic experience for this budding young theologue," Jim Kennedy admits. "Here was a 'non-elect' converted right before my very eyes!"

During those ten days of meetings, some 54 people came forward. "And," Jim adds, "I could have told you who would be coming forward, because I had seen that pastor lead them to Christ during the week!"

"How did you learn to do this?" Jim asked his host.

"In our crusade last year," the minister replied, "we *really* had an evangelist. He took me out with him. I learned by watching him."

Evangelism Explosion Is Born

Jim was an apt pupil. He returned to Ft. Lauderdale a changed person. And what he had seen his minister friend do in Scottdale, Georgia, he began to do in Ft. Lauderdale. Jim began to witness to everyone, and the people in Ft. Lauderdale responded as they had responded in Scottdale.

"After about a year," Jim says, "taking my wife Anne with me—not so much to train her, but because I rarely got to spend time with her—I stopped long enough to remind myself, 'There are a limited number of people I can reach alone. Why not train

Explosion of Evangelism

others to do the same thing?' So I took a man out with me—an elderly man who had been a Christian for about 60 years. He always wanted to lead someone to the Lord, but never knew how. I took him out for months. Finally I 'pushed him out of the nest.' He began to lead a number of people to Christ.

"There was another man whom I took out for a month or so. I went away on vacation, and he called me up the next week and told me he had led someone to Christ. I prayed, 'Lord, maybe this is it. Maybe this is the way.'"

In fact, Jim Kennedy concluded that this *is* the way. "It is what Jesus did. Jesus called His disciples to be with Him so He could show them how to lead others to Him."

As Jim Kennedy put into practice in Ft. Lauderdale what he had seen and tried in Atlanta, people were led into the Kingdom of God and new members joined the little church in the McNab Elementary School. The pain of the downward spiral was forgotten as attendance spurted from 17 to 66—more than enough to charter a fully-organized church.

The following year the charter total almost doubled to a healthy congregation of 122. The little cafetorium was beginning to give them seating problems. The newly finished Kennedy home became virtually "the church," except for Sunday mornings. Anne quickly became proficient in setting up and putting away folding chairs twice a week for evening services on the terrazzo patio. Her mother, back in Lakeland, generously shipped the family piano to meet the need in the new house on 19th Avenue.

Jim Kennedy had found the answer, but the remarkable results led to a new question about how much one man can do. He pondered the possibilities for a long while as he continued to bring new converts into the fold, one at a time. Then, like a bolt of lightning, it hit him. What he needed to do, he realized, was not just to win people to Christ; he needed to train people to win people to Christ. The Bible calls it "equipping the saints" by transferring to them the techniques that work.

"What the church must do," Jim says, "is to get the process of spiritual multiplication going on a worldwide scale. We can do this by training witnesses to train witnesses. That was the way the original witnesses in their day turned the world upside down."

Convinced the church faces the "evangelize or fossilize" alternatives, Jim made the requirement of witness-training a bedrock essential of his ministry. The first effort at training witnesses consisted of a series of classes. Then the trainees were sent out into the community to "try their wings." The results were absolute zero. Even a 25-week training session accomplished no tangible results.

After much prayer and thought, another friendly bolt of lightning struck. "Take your trainees out of the classrooms into the living rooms." The one indispensable ingredient he had overlooked was on-the-job training. Only as the would-be witness goes out with an experienced trainer to observe and then participate does the training really work. Ultimately, that trainee becomes part of the training team, teaching other newcomers how to do it.

It was that simple. Yet it appeared that no one was doing it in an organized, structured way. Jim Kennedy knew that such a training ministry would literally explode the growth patterns of churches, once it was faithfully and intelligently put in practice.

Jim had been a witness to the population explosion—the post-World War II baby boom in America and around the globe. Suddenly the perfect title to his new ministry came to mind. "Evangelism Explosion" describes not the detonation of dynamite but the multiplication of people coming to Christ through the multiplication of trained witnesses empowered by God's Spirit.

It's what had happened in the McNab Elementary School cafetorium. Sunday attendance in excess of 200 packed the place out. It was time to begin planning for the building over on Commercial Boulevard that the Presbytery of the Everglades had set aside for the future Coral Ridge Presbyterian Church.

His life and ministry radically changed, Jim Kennedy now knew he had found the biblical strategy for impacting Ft. Lauderdale, America, and ultimately the world!

God Makes Some Changes in Jim Kennedy

Dr. Thomas H. Stebbins
Executive Vice President, COO

"EE is amazingly logical and clear!"
- Pastor Neil Makris, Greece

"EE has enlarged my heart for the lost."
- Diane Greenwood, USA

Chapter 2

*Evangelism Explosion
Goes Worldwide*

IBM HASN'T DONE it. GM won't do it. The CIA can't do it. But, to the glory of God, a milestone in world evangelism has been achieved. Evangelism Explosion (EE) has been planted in every nation and every territory of the world!

To review the events leading up to this signal achievement, we go back in time a full 40 years to the year EE was officially founded. Once Coral Ridge's new building on Commercial Boulevard was up, attendance continued to escalate. The congregation went from an average Sunday morning attendance of 246 in 1962, the year EE was launched, to 3,134 in 1974. Few members had realized the growth potential their pastor envisioned in the new lay-visitation ministry that was just beginning to crystallize as Evangelism Explosion.

In 1967 Coral Ridge was singled out as the fastest growing church in the denomination and one of the most rapidly expanding in all America. Pastors from every part of the United States were taking note of the rocketing records at Coral Ridge, and they wanted to know Jim Kennedy's secret.

Multiply

At first, Jim tried to respond to each letter, detailing the evangelism principles that God had revealed to him. But the sheer volume of the requests made letter writing impossible. Still, he wanted to help his fellow ministers get their stagnant churches off dead center and multiplying. Here, in Jim Kennedy's words, are the principles:

"The key word is multiply. Our goal in Evangelism Explosion is to raise up a hundred million trained and equipped Christian lay people who are able confidently to share the Gospel of Jesus Christ with others. The New Testament 'secret' of reaching the world for Christ, I repeat, is spiritual multiplication, training witnesses who will train still more witnesses who in turn can train still others.

"The Book of Acts reads that 'there were added 3,000 to the church,' and later, '5,000 more were added.' Then we read that 'the disciples multiplied,' and then, 'they multiplied exceedingly.' It is this shift from addition to spiritual multiplication that offers the one real hope of sharing the Gospel with a world population that is, itself, continually multiplying.

"Evangelism Explosion is transforming the ideal of multiplication into a reality. To the best of my knowledge, there has never been an organization quite like it. First, I had to learn, as a pastor, that I should be witnessing. So I started visiting in the homes of people who had visited our small church. The first two people I led to Christ during Tuesday evening visitation were Anne McDonough and Shirley Engebretsen.

"Next, I realized that I should be training others—my lay people—to witness. In 1962, my wife Anne and those two ladies, together with Victor Wierman and Dr. Freeman Springer, were among the first I trained. In fact, I date the founding of EE to the equipping of my first trainee, Victor Wierman. Then, he and the others helped me train more interested members of our congregation.

"God worked a miracle at Coral Ridge, as first just a few and finally hundreds of lay people were equipped to win people to Christ and to equip others to win people to Christ. That's how our church became the fastest growing church in our denomination.

"Then I discovered a third principle: I needed to train other pastors. So in 1967, we began inviting pastors as well as lay people to the annual clinic. Rev. Archie Parrish and 35 other pastors attended the first one. Archie showed such interest in EE that I asked him to serve as our Minister of Evangelism at Coral Ridge. From 1967 through 1972 we trained 582 pastors and lay leaders in those six clinics.

"When we registered 1,500 pastors and laypeople for our February 1971 clinic, it was evident that demand would soon exceed available space. I also made a fourth discovery: I didn't have to teach all the clinics myself. In 1972, Archie Parrish helped me organize and teach the clinic.

"And that discovery led to a fifth major breakthrough: The clinics did not need to be at Coral Ridge Presbyterian Church in Ft. Lauderdale. In 1973, we held four clinics; three in our church and one in Atlanta, training a total of 269 pastors and lay people.

"But I had already come to one firm conclusion: Our clinics at Coral Ridge 'worked' because trainees could observe what EE, under God, was doing in this church. They could observe my personal enthusiasm and the enthusiasm of our people. They could learn techniques within the context of a healthy local church where lay people have matured through the training process. The venue where the training takes place is very important.

"To avoid EE's becoming only theoretical, all our clinics are taught by people who regularly teach and train in their own churches.

"In 1974, we established three new 'clinic' churches. We held six clinics in all: three at Coral Ridge and three others in Foxboro, Massachusetts; Carrollton, Texas; and San Juan Capistrano, California. In 1975, for the first time, we welcomed internationals to the Coral Ridge clinics: four from Australia, five from England, two from Argentina and one from South Africa.

"The demand for training continued to increase. In 1975 eight clinics were held in the United States: three at Coral Ridge and one each in Philadelphia, Carrollton, Chicago, San Francisco and Portland, certifying a total of 562 graduates. In addition, there were four international clinics: one in Regina, Saskatchewan, one in England, one in South Africa and one in Australia. The number of clinics continued to grow in 1976 and 1977."

EE Gets Its Foothold in the Far East

In 1975, the fall of Vietnam ended missionary service for me (Tom Stebbins) in that country. After an interim assignment on Guam among Vietnamese refugees, I accepted a position as English-speaking pastor at Kowloon Tong Alliance Church in Hong Kong. I loved my congregation, but I sensed that things were not going all that well in the church. Could Evangelism Explosion be the "shot in the arm" the church and I needed?

The clinic in Ft. Lauderdale was an eye-opener for me and a personal revolution. I returned to Hong Kong and announced to Donna, my wife, that I had just experienced "the greatest week of my life!"

Startled a bit by my enthusiasm, Donna asked, "Greater than our honeymoon?"

"Well," I responded, tongue in cheek, "like I said, it was the second greatest week of my life!"

The following year, 1978, we held the first Asia EE clinic at Kowloon Tong Alliance Church. Sixty-four took the course. From Hong Kong the EE ministry spread to Taiwan, the Philippines, Korea, Singapore, Malaysia and other Asian nations. EE had attained a solid following in East Asia.

For ten years the number of international clinics continued to multiply. In 1984 the international clinics (43) outnumbered those held in the United States (25)! Two years later there were 36 clinics in the United States and 104 elsewhere. Again the international clinics far exceeded the number held at home.

Every Nation

In November 1988, Jim Kennedy reported to the EE Board: "I have asked the vice presidents to set a goal for getting the EE ministry into every country of the world by 1995. That is, I want us to have at least one EE church in every nation training its people in personal evangelism. I have asked them to lay out a strategy with the following steps:

- To determine how many nations there are in the world
- To determine how many nations we are presently in
- To determine how many nations we will need to enter in the next seven years to accomplish this goal
- To lay out a plan for each year indicating which countries we will enter that year

Explosion of Evangelism

- To monitor our progress according to this plan"

After careful research, the vice presidents determined that at that time there were 211 nations in the world, and that according to their records, EE was in 66 nations. They added, on the basis of their research, that getting EE into every nation might "prove impossible" for two reasons:

1. There was no Christian church in some nations and EE historically works only through churches. This problem was resolved by modifying the criteria. Instead of saying "at least one church," they would say "at least one EE-trained believer training another believer through EE to witness and train others as well."
2. Some nations outlawed evangelism totally. *Operation World* reported that several nations EE had hoped to enter strictly forbad evangelizing and proselytizing. The vice presidents concluded their very realistic report to the Board with these words: "We will appreciate the Board's praying for us as we push towards our 1995 goal. Prayer can change the world! Pray!"

And with that, the vice presidents rolled up their sleeves and went to work to change the world.

As the regional vice presidents pressed forward on their goal of "every nation," they reported miracle after miracle. A Chinese layman in Singapore traveled to China. Covertly he conducted a five-day EE clinic, training a score of pastors and lay people. He told them, "Now go back home and for the next 16 weeks train your church to witness to their friends, family, neighbors and fellow farmers."

The teacher intended for them to do this a few hours each

Evangelism Explosion Goes Worldwide

week. But they misunderstood him to say that they should witness all day, every day for sixteen weeks! The result? Those EE trained Christians witnessed to 30,000 people and saw 20,000 of them converted! That's spiritual multiplication!

By 1990 (less than two full years after Jim Kennedy's directive to the vice presidents), the number of nations that EE was reaching with the Gospel dramatically increased to 103. In 1992 Russia opened to EE and other nations were added for a total of 141 nations. By 1994 EE continued its worldwide impact with a presence in 174 nations. In January 1996 EE miraculously entered the final and most difficult nation of all—North Korea.

On March 17, 1996, in Ft. Lauderdale, there was an impressive celebration at Coral Ridge Presbyterian Church. Representatives marched down the center aisle with 211 national flags as EE President/Founder D. James Kennedy read off the names of the nations amid grateful applause to God. EE had been planted in every nation!

As Jim Kennedy came to Zaire (formerly Belgium Congo) in his alphabetical reading, he paused. "Thirty-some years ago," he announced, "I applied to go as a missionary to this country. For health reasons that wasn't possible. But today, through EE and by God's grace, I've been able to minister there at last!" Applause and cheers rose in a sustained crescendo!

Someone noted with praise to God that more national flags were present and more countries were represented than at any other function in history. Not even the Olympics, not even the United Nations had such a diversity.

. . . and Territory

It wasn't long until EE leaders, staff and people were asking,

"What's next?" Jim Kennedy reminded us that there were still many territories where EE also needed to be planted. Territories with hard-to-pronounce names like Andaman-Nicabar, Lakshadweep, Tokelau. Territories, though a part of a country or empire, do not have the full status of a state or province. But these territories were also a part of "the ends of the earth" (Acts 1:8) in need of the Gospel.

By the year 2000, one territory remained unreached by EE—Tokelau, a remote group of islands northeast of Australia. Establishing a base on Tokelau was not easy. Boat travel to Tokelau was infrequent, and the Islanders needed face-to-face dialogue. At last two very dedicated EE field workers from Fiji traveled to Western Samoa and then on to Tokelau. One of them resigned his job to make the long trip. These two workers remained on Tokelau for five weeks to train believers in EE. They also prepared for a clinic to help local churches implement the EE ministry.

But to give a fuller account of EE's expansion into every nation and territory of the world, we need to elaborate on several other crucial aspects of the story: EE's leadership, materials, finance, facilities, difficulties, triumphs and endorsements.

Leadership

If a leader is a person who influences his followers to achieve a purpose, Jim Kennedy is unquestionably a leader of the first order. Not only did he lead the charge to take the ministry into every nation and territory, but he has gathered around him a group of committed men and women who have contributed immensely to the objective.

Through the years Jim Kennedy has been assisted by a series of executive vice presidents:

- Rev. Archie Parrish was the first in a line of six men. Archie, a great administrator, teacher, motivator and discipler, was influential in advancing the ministry of EE beyond the limits of Fort Lauderdale.
- Rev. T. M. Moore was used of God to refine the Evangelism Explosion textbook, training notebook and supplemental materials.
- Dr. Woody Lajara brought to the ministry great charisma, first-hand experience and fund-raising skills.
- At a time when EE's explosive growth brought extreme financial stress, Mr. Merlin Feather, with his years of experience in banking, rescued the ministry from financial disaster.
- Rev. E.H. (Buddy) Gaines, with many years of overseas experience and graduate studies in missiology, saw to it that the EE ministry and materials were indigenized as the overseas emphasis expanded.
- In 1995, Jim Kennedy honored me, Tom Stebbins, to serve in this position of EE leadership.

Two other EE leaders have played a pivotal role in EE's success: John Sorensen, Vice President for Ministry Advancement and Derek Kelmanson, Vice President for Finance and Operations. I first met John in my office while still pastoring at Christ Community Church in Omaha, Nebraska. John was a despondent, young man who had tried just about everything and was about ready to give up on life. After I heard him share in detail about his family background and his occupational skills, I said, "John, if you will put your life in God's hands, He will meet your every need and use you beyond your wildest dreams!"

"How does one do that?" John replied. Using the EE outline, I shared the Gospel with him. Before I knew it, John was on his knees trusting Christ as his Lord and Savior. Shortly after, he led his fiancée, Ann, to Christ. Then I had the joy of mentoring John and training both of them in EE. John accompanied me on a short-term missions trip to Barbados in the Caribbean and caught the vision to serve Christ in missions.

When I moved to Fort Lauderdale in July 1995, John was upset that I would abandon him. Shortly after that, he phoned and asked if he could come to Fort Lauderdale to attend a Leadership Training Clinic to become a lay teacher trainer. Since our guest room was occupied he happily slept on our couch, video taped the clinic and went home convinced that he should move to Fort Lauderdale. Later, he called and told me he was being offered a position in Chicago and another in Los Angeles at a six-figure salary, but he would prefer to work for EE at less than half that salary.

John started by producing videos, newsletters, and anything else we needed him to do. Today, John has almost completed a Masters in Evangelism, has been ordained, and is our Vice President for Ministry Advancement. He is leading the way in fund-raising for the ministry and helping other team members raise their personal support. If anyone questions whether EE works, they need to meet John!

While John was worshipping and fellowshipping at Coral Ridge Presbyterian Church, he met a fine young deacon named Derek, who from a teenager and throughout college had been active in EE. When they struck up a friendship, John learned Derek had a wealth of experience as financial officer in his father-in-law's business. He was in charge of the warehouse and marketing. John sensed that he had the exact qualifications needed in our Operations Department.

One day, when there was an opening as Vice President for

Evangelism Explosion Goes Worldwide

Finance and Operations, John recommended Derek to me. Everyone on staff praises God for bringing Derek to our leadership team. He has been a wonderful "God send" and has kept EE in the black at all times. Like John, Derek is EE-trained, an avid personal evangelist and trainer.

Gladys Israels, whom Jim Kennedy led to Christ and trained in EE, has been a loyal part of the team these past 40 years. For a year and a half, as the ministry was getting its start, she met weekly with Archie Parrish, Jim Carlson and Mike Dempsy. During those two-and-a-half-hour lunches at Brave Bull Restaurant on Federal Highway, this "executive committee" (before it was called that) laid the groundwork for EE. These four extremely committed people drafted a master plan that included the preparation of materials, the conducting of training clinics and the taking of EE to other cities. When EE was officially incorporated in 1970, Gladys became the Board's first secretary, an office she still holds today.

Twice the Board has been enlarged. In 1977 it was enlarged to include other evangelical denominations, and in 1981 to include the international directors. Today Dr. Kennedy chairs a 29-member Board, 2 from each of the seven continents and 14 from the United States.

The ministry on each of the seven continents is led by a continental vice president. Continents are divided into regions led by regional coordinators or directors. In many overseas countries, the ministry is led by a national director and an advisory board.

Materials

Evangelism Explosion, the basic textbook for EE, was first published in 1970. Later, Archie Parrish added a training notebook and supplemental booklets to be used in both the clinics and in the local churches.

A major undertaking for EE has been the translation and publishing of these materials in other languages. Translation Agreements insure that the essential Gospel message is faithfully conveyed. A limited printing is field-tested before the materials are mass produced in a given language. Because of the large amount of Scripture in EE materials, they adapt well in almost every culture.

A recent innovation is the wordless flip chart, effective in a witness to illiterate or semi-literate people. The silhouette figures in the "Do You Know for Sure" tract, so generic in their style, can be used effectively in any culture to explain the Gospel. This has opened an opportunity to witness to and train people who heretofore have been passed by.

Finances

Next to leadership and appropriate materials, money ranks near the top of the "needs" list in any ministry. When EE has had sufficient money, it has advanced rapidly. When the money has been lacking, it has struggled.

From day one, profits from the sale of materials and receipts from well attended leadership training clinics have been accompanied by sacrificial and generous donations.

People who have found Christ through EE, who have seen their lives changed through EE's equipping ministry, reach for their wallets or checkbooks. People who watch their church grow through the impact of EE are eager to support the ministry worldwide.

Martha Winter, age 104, lived with her daughter Marjorie in Glenwood, Iowa. She could not very well board a plane and fly to Albania or Brazil to participate in an EE clinic.

But Martha and Marjorie faithfully prayed and faithfully gave. By their prayer and gifts, they had a worldwide impact.

Hundreds of Christians have participated in the "Committee of a Thousand" to support EE with thousand-dollar gifts or more every year. Others, including youth and children, their resources more limited, have stuffed our blue plastic fish banks with coins.

When the banks are full, they send us checks sometimes for as much as a hundred dollars!

On several occasions, following the home-going of EE friends, we have received large gifts from their estates. On two occasions just this past year, we were faced with large shortfalls that threatened to curtail EE's ministry. Both times, a sizeable gift from an estate met the financial need. Both times it was almost the exact amount needed to wipe out the deficit.

Through the years several Christian organizations have supported our ministries, generously providing funds for projects which we otherwise could never have attempted. But probably the greatest resource that has impacted EE's growth and worldwide expansion is the large number, hundreds of thousands (maybe millions!), of unpaid volunteers who have given of their time and efforts to serve in EE.

Their work has made EE cost-effective. One of our financial officers calculated, by dividing the dollar amount of our annual budget by the number of people led to Christ in a given year, that for the past four years we have seen someone profess faith in Jesus Christ for every $1.21 given to the ministry. Is any other ministry that cost-effective?

About five years ago, EE was going through a severe money crisis. After an extended time of fasting and prayer, I asked all of our vice presidents and many of our directors to begin raising money toward their personal salaries. It was not easy. None of us had any experience in that type of fund-raising. But God helped us. We were able to find some new resources. God has provided.

There is another reason why EE International can impact the world for so few dollars. Increasingly, the overseas ministries have become self-supporting. They are paying the salaries of their own staff, financing their own training clinics, printing their own materials and even supporting their own EE missionaries as they take the Gospel and the training ministry to other nations.

Facilities

From the start of its ministry, EE International rented office space. First it was on McNab Road in Pompano, then in another location on McNab Road and today on the third floor of Knox Building across the street from Coral Ridge Presbyterian Church. On a number of occasions EE leaders have considered buying or building, but we prefer to rent at our present location and invest the money God has entrusted to us in direct ministry.

Whether we rent or own, we have found it important for a national ministry to have a headquarters. Jose Carlos Ribeiro, national director for EE Brazil, expressed it this way:

"First, having our own national office will give us an interdenominational image. Though the Baptist church in Sao Paulo has generously provided us an office, too many Christians here assume that EE serves only Baptists.

"Second," Ribiero continued, "if we have our own office, churches in Brazil will know we are here to stay. And third, our growing ministry has an increasing need for adequate space to store and dispense our materials. The church where we are now can't possibly provide this for us."

In Chapter One we saw how God sovereignly chose a person, Jim Kennedy, to direct an evangelistic endeavor that was destined to carry Christ's name to the far corners of earth.

This chapter has briefly looked at that worldwide development of Evangelism Explosion.

Chapter Three will look in greater detail at the many aspects of EE in North America. Then, succeeding chapters will recount how EE was established on the other six continents: South America, the Carribean, Europe, Asia, Africa, Australia and the Pacific Islands. It's an exciting story worthy of your time!

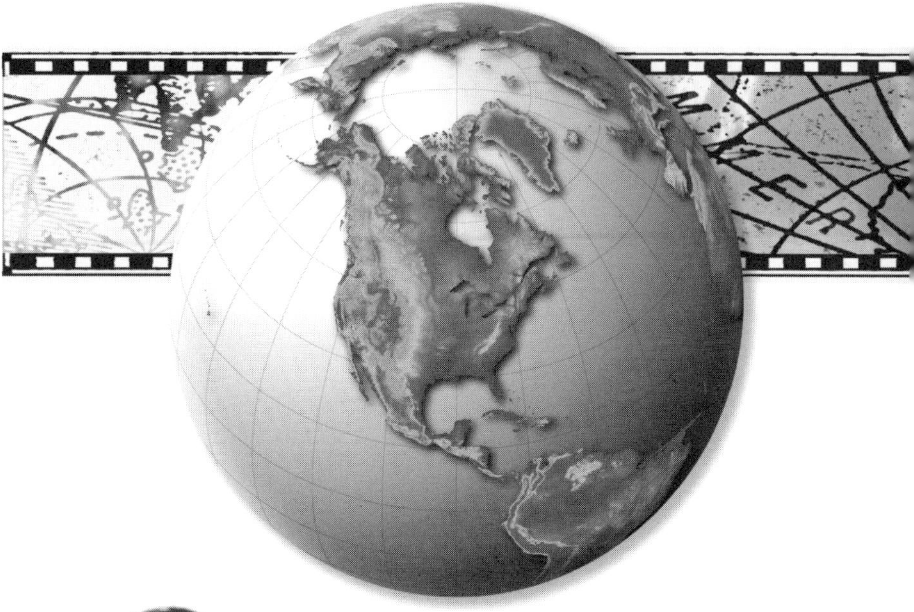

North America
Rev. Ray Castro
Vice President, North America

"Through EE, God has shown me the urgency of sharing the Gospel with those around me."
- Jim Reichhoff, USA

"I've come to anticipate those opportunities I once feared!"
- Chuck Lovell, USA

Chapter 3

North America: Evangelism Begins at Home

IN OUR QUEST to change the world, we knew one thing was certain. Before EE could change the world, it was essential that those of us involved in EE do our part by God's power, grace and wisdom, to bring about spiritual change in our home base—North America.

Dr. R. C. Sproul, noted theologian and author, comes to Fort Lauderdale regularly to teach courses at Knox Theological Seminary (Knox is located on the first floor of the Knox Building). On one of those regular trips to Fort Lauderdale, he had a few hours between classes and came up the elevator to our headquarters for a visit. I was honored and surprised that he would spend more than an hour with me in my office, and when he explained the reason for his visit, I wasn't just surprised—I was exhilarated!

Dr. Sproul wanted to share with me how much EE had meant to him and his ministry. More than 20 years earlier he had attended one of our leadership training clinics at Coral Ridge Presbyterian Church. Upon his return home to Ohio, he trained about 250 other people. "From there," R.C. said, "the laity involved caught the vision for ministry, and people began their own specialized ministries to prisoners, the poor, the unemployed and those needing marriage counseling."

Thousands of similar testimonies about EE's impact—changing lives, ministries and whole churches throughout North America—could be included if we had time and space in this brief chapter. How can one in such limited space do justice to all God has done on this continent in these past forty years? In this brief history of EE in North America, many stories of multiplication and triumph will necessarily be left untold. But here is at least a sampling of what God has done—under eight headings. First, what He has done and continues to do through . . .

Local Churches

According to our purpose statement, EE aims to "glorify God by equipping believers in and through local churches to multiply worldwide." EE in North America—and on every other continent—is local church-based and local church-centered. We do not see EE as a para-church ministry. EE was born in a local church, developed in a local church, proven eminently successful in local churches and continues—across America and Canada—to focus 95 percent of its ministry in and through local churches.

In the last chapter you read the story of Coral Ridge Presbyterian Church, where EE got started. Here are now the testimonies of God's blessing through EE upon other local churches in three other denominations.

Bellevue Baptist is an historic church where Dr. Adrian Rogers serves as senior pastor. Dr. Rogers writes, "Thanks to EE we have 1,500 trained witnesses here at Bellevue. We are

North America: Evangelism Begins at Home

seeing people saved every week and added to this great church."

EE was launched in that church by a lay teacher trainer, Larry Piedt, a pilot for Northwest Airlines who moved from South Florida to Memphis in 1986. His family joined Bellevue, and under the leadership of Dr. Rogers, he began to teach EE in the church.

The EE ministry grew from one team in level one to 135 teams in seven levels of training. In 11 years EE teams had made 32,476 contacts in the community and 2,710 people prayed to receive Christ in those 11 years. In one year alone, 315 persons professed their faith in Christ. In July 1993, under Larry's leadership, Bellevue hosted their first EE clinic with 50 clinicians, and the church has become a bastion of EE training ever since.

Rev. Mike Coppersmith, pastor of Our Savior's Lutheran Church in Palm Springs, California, invested a week in an EE clinic. He wanted to find out if EE would help him train his congregation to lead others to Christ. He began by training one team. Because the senior pastor was leading the charge, interest and participation increased, and before long there were 12 three-member teams sharing the Gospel. In two semesters of training, 68 people accepted Christ as Lord and Savior.

Every four months, 30 to 60 new members were received into the church, and worship service attendance has grown beyond the limits of the church's 300-seat sanctuary. A Director for Discipleship has been added to the staff to help conserve the results and fold the new believers into the church. Other churches are beginning to ask what's happening at Our Savior's Lutheran. The answer is found in Acts 2:47: "And the Lord was adding to their number day by day those who were being saved."

Pastor Jorge Comesañas at First Baptist (Hispanic) Church in Coral Park, Miami, Florida, at first didn't realize that EE is interdenominational. Sixteen years ago, just looking for fellowship with other pastors, he attended an EE clinic. In his words, "I came back with a dream about the future of my church." He shared with his congregation his vision of using EE to reach out into the community. "There was so much interest that I had to send my wife to Puerto Rico to be trained to assist me."

Upon her return from that clinic, their EE ministry was launched. The results transcended anything they could have imagined. Pastor Comesañas was passionate in his resolve to implement EE regularly: "Didn't matter whether we had tornado warnings or hurricanes, we were faithful. And every single week we were reaching people." He added that since they started EE 12 years ago, their church has never had a week where they didn't have a decision for Christ.

EE created a "new, fresh spirit" among the members. "When you are using evangelism as a lifestyle, as EE teaches, the members concentrate on other people's needs instead of their own," explained Pastor Comesañas. "It's a healthy congregation when you have soul winning as a way of life."

Now, 12 years later, his church has exploded to 2,000 members and is growing fast! "We're baptizing people every week," said Pastor Comesañas.

Another pastor who accompanied Pastor Comesañas to that EE clinic 12 years ago also had a congregation of 150. Unlike Pastor Comesañas, he did not implement EE in his church. Today that pastor's congregation is still at 150.

Pastor Comesañas adds excitedly, "I have to tell other pastors and leaders in the community that this tool is from the Bible. It's from God and it's working!"

Leadership Training Clinics

If the local church is the centerpiece of EE, clinics are the launching pad and the spreading device for EE, because it's at clinics where pastors are inspired and equipped to launch the EE ministry in their local churches.

Rick Fisher heard about Evangelism Explosion at a Saturday morning breakfast meeting. Within weeks, Rick and one of the pastors from his church signed up for the clinic at First Baptist Church, Dallas, Texas. Rick was amazed to hear clinic teacher Charles Thornton describe the success of his 20-year EE ministry at First Baptist in Euless, Texas. Rick said, "He is an awesome individual. I hope and pray that I can serve and glorify God the way Charles does."

During the clinic, Rick's enthusiasm grew even more as he saw 75 people come to Christ through three nights of on-the-job training. "I have never experienced such an intensely spiritual event," exclaimed Rick, "I have forever been changed!"

Clinic "base" churches that have adequate facilities and an active quality EE ministry host clinics. Preparation for the clinic begins at least four months in advance. Adult clinics offer approximately 37 hours of training in five days. One or two experienced and certified clinic teachers, who have an active and fruitful ministry in their own church, lead the clinics.

Certified trainers from the clinic base church demonstrate various parts of the EE presentation in the classroom and take the clinicians in teams of three for on-the-job training experience in homes, malls, laundromats, parks, etc. At the close of the clinic, pastors and lay leaders who satisfactorily complete the training are awarded a teacher/trainer certificate which qualifies them to launch and lead a quality EE ministry in their church.

From the first clinic held in Fort Lauderdale taught by Dr. Kennedy and attended by 36 clinicians, the clinic ministry grew to four US clinics in 1973, six clinics in 1974 and eight clinics in 1975. By then, the clinics had spread to other cities. In addition to three clinics being held in Fort Lauderdale, churches in Philadelphia, Carrolton (Dallas, TX area), Chicago, San Francisco and Portland also hosted clinics, maintaining the same quality and procedures. The number of US clinics continued to grow to 10 in 1978, 14 in 1979, 22 in 1980, 29 in 1981 and 34 in 1983. The number of these clinics in North America continues to increase.

EE has always sought to add innovative training approaches while maintaining the same basic principles in regular clinics. Hence, in 1982, Pastor Don DeKok, in Bismark, North Dakota, began hosting and teaching clinics for pastors of small churches in small communities. Covenant Seminary in St. Louis, cooperating with a local EE church in that city, offered EE training for prospective pastors. Alliance Theological Seminary in Nyack, New York, offered a five-day May Term EE clinic complete with on-the-job training and proper certification.

Pastors and lay people are always excited to experience the impact of such clinics on their own lives and on their churches when they return home. One recent clinician named Jim exclaimed to me over lunch, "EE really works! I've been praying for years for a ministry like this. It's a non-offensive way to give a clear and concise Gospel presentation to anyone."

Jim went on to tell me that this all started for him when only two months earlier, he and his wife Mimi traveled from Mississippi to vacation in Fort Lauderdale. Jim explained, "We were driving by Coral Ridge Church and decided to stop in for a visit. In the bookstore I purchased one of your books on evan-

North America: Evangelism Begins at Home

gelism. In your book you kept referring to Evangelism Explosion and the blessing it had been to you. So I called your office to find out more. The person I talked to suggested I attend an EE clinic and bring my pastor.

"During the clinic I personally led two people to Christ. Then on the way home I stopped to visit a friend. For two years I had tried to witness to him. This time he listened and in tears prayed to receive Christ as his Savior. Since then, to God's glory, my pastor, my wife and I have led 36 people to Christ. Our little church in Mississippi, after twenty-some years of non-growth, is beginning to show signs of life!"

What Jim shared with me over lunch that day is taking place all over this continent and on every continent of the world! Another basic factor in EE's success and spread across this continent is its quality . . .

Advanced Seminars

To improve existing EE ministries in local churches, EE North America has offered Advanced Seminars in various key centers across the continent. The seminars are generally held from Friday noon or evening through Saturday and are open for anyone to attend for a modest registration that covers meals and materials.

Experienced clinic teachers or EE staff present workshops on various subjects like Follow-up, Prospecting, Enlistment, EE in the Sunday School, EE in the Small Town, Dealing with Cults, Introduction to Advance Levels and more.

At the close of one such seminar, one layman/trainer from Virginia Beach wrote, "I needed every area discussed." A pastor from Charlottesville, Virginia, commented, "A wealth of experience . . . very practical. Excellent motivation for organizing and implementing!" And another pastor from Lake Wales, Florida, remarked, "We needed a booster shot in the arm. The Advanced Seminar is just what we needed."

One more recent workshop has dealt with a strategy to help the laity in local churches take some of the administrative load off their pastors. The workshop is called "STEAM," an acronym, each letter of which stands for one of five key areas of focus: Supplication, Teaching, Enlistment, Administration and Maintaining Records. A team of five lay leaders are equipped in the workshop, each one to coordinate one of these areas in the EE ministry of their local church.

After implementing this strategy in his church, Pastor Chris Beam in North Houston, Texas, wrote, "Yes, we have a STEAM Team.... The workshop enlarged our vision and gave opportunity to hear many ideas of how people are leading their EE ministries with STEAM teams. Personally, I couldn't lead our EE ministry without our STEAM Team. They are dedicated to equipping our members with better skills to witness. They help organize EE strategies for the coming semester and provide counsel in assigning trainers and trainees to teams. I strongly suggest that every pastor seek God in prayer for the right people to develop a STEAM Team."

Leadership

Every ministry is a reflection of its leadership. This is especially true at EE. Jim Kennedy has been a marvelous example of faithfulness, commitment and passion. Though he has always been an extremely busy pastor, from the very first days of EE, he has taught EE classes and taken teams of three into the community for on-the-job training. Three times a year he has done the same at his church's EE clinics. Jim is a leader of vision, faith, perseverance and gifted administration.

But as he said earlier in this book, he soon learned that he couldn't do everything himself. So he began to train and delegate to other faithful men who could help him lead the ministry. Rev. Archie Parrish, who served as Minister of Evangelism at Coral Ridge, also became the first (what we would call today) Vice President for North America. Archie, like his mentor, Jim, also became an exemplary, passionate, and visionary leader.

But, as his responsibilities expanded overseas, and he assumed international leadership, it was necessary for him to delegate North America to Rev. Mike Carlisle. In 1984, after several years of able leadership, Mike moved on to take a pastorate, and Rev. David Clippard was appointed to the post. David greatly impacted EE across America and launched an Advanced Seminar ministry where EE pastors and lay people could receive further training to help them implement EE effectively in their churches. But David missed the pastorate greatly, so in 1988 he moved to Sarasota, Florida, and built a strong EE church there.

David was followed by Rev. Tommy Hinson, who brought many years of fruitful EE and pastoral leadership to the helm of EE North America. Tommy was instrumental in bringing a total revision of EE's training materials and cast the vision for appointing volunteer field workers to help pastors implement quality EE ministries in their churches.

For a few years after Tommy retired in 1995, the responsibilities were covered by the Executive Vice President until, at last, Rev. Shelby A. Smith, Jr., was appointed to the position of Vice President for North America.

Shelby, ministering out of his home in Smyrna, Tennessee, was a strong field leader enlisting, training and assigning four

US Regional Coordinators (RC) with responsibility to "enlist pastors and lay people into EE training and help their churches to implement the EE ministry." Rev. Fred Kress serves as the RC for the Northeast Region, Rev. Les Morgan in the Southeast Region, Rev. Jim Fryer in the Midwest and Rev. Clint Pruett in the South Central.

In the year 2000, Shelby accepted a position at the Southern Baptist Sunday school in Nashville, and Rev. Ray Castro accepted the position and has added many needed refinements to the ministry. Ray has a wonderful vision with strategies for increasing the number of clinics and churches involved in EE.

Materials

EE's training materials, from the beginning, have been marked by excellence. Initially, Dr. Kennedy distributed to his trainees a two-page bare-bones outline. Gradually, lecture notes were added and finally, the textbook *Evangelism Explosion* was published. Gradually, Archie Parrish added a training notebook and three supplemental booklets for follow-up, enlistment and prayer partners.

In 1983, EE revised all the materials, but they were soon felt to be too complex. The next year a five-year plan was drafted for a more thorough revision. Twenty clinic teachers and leaders were asked to evaluate the existing materials and submit recommendations for changes. After these were received and carefully evaluated, the men were invited to Fort Lauderdale for face-to-face discussions to arrive at a consensus regarding needed revisions.

David Clippard completed a first draft of the new materials. This first draft was sent out to twenty churches for field testing. Using the evaluations and suggestions from the field test churches, and while still serving as Outreach Pastor of Christ Community Church in Omaha, Nebraska, I rewrote the first draft, expanding, reformatting and augmenting the teaching notes and transparencies. I also revised the supplemental materials and wrote and published the first EE tract entitled "Do You Know for Sure?"

In May 1988, when Tommy Hinson assumed the position of Vice President, he spent hundreds of hours rewriting, reformatting, coordinating and correlating the newly revised materials and took them to the publisher. Pastor Greg Elmquist commented about the new revision that they had "lowered the level of frustration resulting in trainee drop-outs, while at the same time increasing the percentage of returning trainers." Pastor Charles Thornton wrote, "Learning the material in chronological order is a great benefit, and having the lecture outline in front of each trainee is a big plus."

Ten years transpired before it was felt the materials needed their most recent revision. Pastor Jim Engle, Director of Evangelism at Coral Ridge, and one of the top clinic teachers, was assigned the task. Materials were again field-tested. And the new 2000 Level I Training Notebook was highly acclaimed the best ever.

The new materials are lauded for the following reasons: 1) the notes are simplified by 30 percent to allow adequate class time for teaching, 2) the notebook is packaged in a beautiful four-color new-look spiral binding, 3) state-of-the-art graphics for a PowerPoint™ presentation or transparencies make the lectures come alive and 4) a new diploma and lapel pin is given to every trainee completing the training. In the not-too-distant future, Level II and III training notes will also be revised.

Self Analysis and Refinement

From the earliest years, EE has constantly sought to evaluate, refine and innovate. Even before the ministry was known as EE, Jim and Anne Kennedy would come back from their witnessing visits and compare notes, discuss how they might have answered tough questions better and refined the outline to preclude meeting those objections again.

Beginning with the earliest clinics, at the end of every lecture there was then, and is today, an evaluation sheet where clinicians are asked to critique the lecture content and the presentation of the lecturer. These evaluations are forwarded to the clinic office, read carefully and suggestions recorded and forwarded to those in leadership.

A generous donor, wishing to remain anonymous, made possible a 1992 North American Ministries Self-Analysis. It was held in Atlanta, Georgia, March 27-28, 1992. Twelve of Evangelism Explosion's most knowledgeable and involved leaders in North America immersed themselves in this study for two full days. This resulted in 44 "action statements" which could be divided logically into four categories:

1. To help increase clinic attendance
2. To improve clinicians' ministry implementation following clinics
3. To involve new sources of financial support
4. To guide the North American ministry in general matters

In 1996, we engaged the services of David Schmidt and Associates in Wheaton, Illinois, to survey hundreds of churches now active in EE and an equal number of churches no longer active. We wanted to know what the churches were saying EE was doing well and what we might do better. Six recommendations emerged from the survey:

1. Simplify the ministry
2. Shorten the ministry
3. Teach people flexibility in sharing their faith
4. Teach relational skills
5. Emphasize discipleship and follow-up more
6. Redesign EE materials to be more attractive and user friendly

The following year we hosted a consultation of major church and denominational leaders in evangelism in Fort Lauderdale. We wanted further input on how we could make EE more effective and relevant to today's American church and society. The recommendations from these surveys and consultations were given serious consideration and most, if not all, of the recommendations were implemented in EE's ministry. This brought many favorable comments and reactions from churches across the continent.

Trials and Testing

While God has granted to EE North America innumerable triumphs, we have also experienced some very difficult tests and trials. Financial shortages present to the staff and ministry frequent moments of stress. Yet through 40 years, God has provided, and the ministry continues to grow and bear abundant fruit. Here is just one of the trials that has impacted the ministry:

On December 15, 1979, a terrible hot air balloon accident occurred when three EE-trained men in Fort Lauderdale lost their lives.

Early that Saturday morning, Jack Mowday, Glen Berg and Rick Rhine—all insurance agents, members of Coral Ridge Presbyterian Church and EE trainers—rose early to go for a hot air balloon ride. This was a surprise Christmas gift from Jack's wife, Lois. Two wives, Lois and Gail Berg and fiancée Kathy Divincenzo followed the air balloon in a station wagon.

Suddenly, the hot air balloon hit some electric wires. As the balloon basket caught fire, Jack, Glen and Rick jumped out of the balloon and fell to their immediate death. Lois, Gail, and Kathy witnessed the whole accident and knew that the three men were transported instantly into God's presence.

Jack and Lois had been led to Christ earlier by an EE team from the church. All six of them were active in EE and looking for opportunities to share their faith.

When a young man from the balloon company asked how this could happen, Kathy had a golden opportunity to share with him the message of eternal life. The other women joined her in sharing the Gospel with bystanders at the accident.

The three women each testified that the men were ready to meet the Lord and that they were strong in their faith because of their training and experience in EE. This testimony of God's grace in the midst of tragedy led to numerous speaking, writing and witnessing opportunities.

Prayer

Prayer is a crucial part of EE, not only when we meet trials and tests, but in advancing the ministry on every front. In 1976 Archie Parrish initiated the Prayer Partner ministry whereby at the beginning of every semester, each teacher, trainer or trainee enlists two prayer partners to pray for him or her throughout the semester, especially on the evening of on-the-job training. EE participants meet with their prayer partners face-to-face for at least fifteen minutes every week. Then, after the report session, the EE participants call their prayer partners to inform them regarding the results of the night of visiting and witnessing.

At the end of the first semester of prayer partner support, the results were tallied, and to everyone's amazement, there had been a 100 percent increase in the number of professions. Archie also prepared a little booklet we now call *Partners in Prayer*. In addition to marvelous answers to prayer, this new prayer strategy has brought another significant benefit. Having prayed for EE for 13 straight weeks, their interest in and excitement about EE grows, and they become the best candidates for next semester's enlistment.

Bernie and Alice Cull take EE teams into gang-infested areas of Phoenix, Arizona. Before they share the Gospel, their first priority is prayer. "Without prayer," Bernie remarks, "there'd be little help for us." But backed by prayer, Bernie and Alice have experienced God's grace. In 1994, their EE teams saw 2,226 professions for Christ. In 1995, the number grew to 3,218, and in 1996 to 4,208. Now in their 80's this elderly couple are still seeing astounding results as a result of prayer.

Our experience at the EE headquarters is similar. We note that where there's no prayer, there's also no blessing; little prayer, little blessing; much prayer, great blessing. At one point in my first few years of leadership at EE our Vice President for Finance informed me that our cash balance was almost depleted and we were on course to close our doors in about three weeks. Not being a financial genius, I felt there was only one thing to do, and I had never before done it: fast and pray.

In fact, I felt so desperate that I lay face down on the floor of my house and cried out to God for help. For two weeks I went without food and prayed earnestly for God's intervention. God began to give unusual wisdom. He sent some very unexpected ministry partners our way. He gave us the courage to cut back drastically on expenses, and He opened our eyes to some new resources. In answer to prayer, He saved the ministry from financial disaster.

Our entire staff began to set aside one day every quarter when we close the office, go to a nearby church and fast and pray. Amazing things have happened. God has raised up quality staff to lead new branches of ministry. He has supplied financial grants for new projects. He opened doors to inaccessible nations. And recently, our Executive Committee approved our setting aside one day worldwide every year specially designated for—prayer.

Thus far in this book I have focused primarily on our standard EE adult ministry. In recent years, however, EE has branched out into new fields such as Youth EE, Kids' EE, Seniors' EE, Prison EE, Intercultural EE, as well as EE in Canada. The development and growth of these ministries demands a chapter of their own. Hence, I invite you to read about these exciting innovations in the next chapter.

North America: Evangelism Begins at Home

Rev. Rick Bond
VP, Youth EE

Rev. Robert Foster
Dir., Intercultural EE

Dr. Karen Gushta
Dir., Kids' EE

Rev. Art Hallett
Dir., Prison EE

Mr. Larry Piedt
Dir., Seniors' EE

"After once using Seniors' EE in a nursing home, I was hooked!"
- Bev Wallhoff, USA

"Youth EE has brought excitement to our teens. It has totally turned our youth group around."
- Josh Edmonds, USA

Chapter 4

The Gospel Is for Everyone

A FEW YEARS back we scheduled a Leadership Advance (we refuse to call them "retreats") for our seven Continental and three Divisional Vice Presidents. During our time together, we crafted a "Vision 2000" statement. It sums up what we feel God wants EE to accomplish before Christ's return. You might call it our concept of how EE can best complete Christ's Great Commission. This is it:

> *Every nation equipping every people group and every age group to witness to every person.*

Subsequently our International Board as well approved the statement. This statement means that in North America, in addition to our work with adults generally, we will witness to and equip youth, kids, seniors. We also will share the Gospel with and train prison inmates and the many intercultural people living among us.

In this chapter we will look at how EE, in its brief 40-year history, has been changing the lives of those within these other categories and more.

Youth EE

"Because of Youth EE, evangelism has become a part of my comfort zone," says Lauren Fielding, at the time a teenager. "I have grown closer to God. EE really does change our world!"

Youth Pastor Greg Soulder concurs. "God is using Youth EE as a ministry tool and a catalyst to spark revival in our church. I love the Youth EE outline."

"But," you may ask, "what's the difference between Youth EE and Adult EE?"

Simply put, Youth EE is more user friendly for young people. Both courses have the same basic Gospel outline, but the wording, the style, the transitions and illustrations are more youth oriented. Not that it's written in some sort of hip, adolescent vernacular. Rather, it's less formal. It expresses the Gospel using phrases with which younger people are comfortable.

Youth EE traces its roots back to 1976 when John Musselman came to serve as Minister of Youth at Coral Ridge Presbyterian Church. At the time he was working on his Doctor of Ministry degree. John asked Jim Kennedy if he might prepare a Youth EE Gospel presentation for his dissertation. He field-tested the presentation by using it to train the church youth. In the space of five years almost 500 students were trained at Coral Ridge in Youth EE.

John next developed a junior high-level program ten weeks in length, but otherwise very similar to the high school training model. Junior high youth did not become trainers because they couldn't yet drive. Young adults had to serve in that role.

In 1981 John held the first Youth EE clinic at Coral Ridge.

The Gospel Is for Everyone

By 1996, he had trained 120 youth pastors in the youth clinics held there. Another 75 youth pastors received training in other clinics.

"We are involved in training youth pastors to train high school students and junior high students," John says. "One of the exciting aspects of this ministry is that we are training the leaders of tomorrow. The preparation for life-style evangelism these students receive is incredible. We are preparing a generation of students who don't have to wait until they are adults to know how to share their faith.

"In college, some of our students have been asked by local churches to be on the evangelism committee because they know more about evangelism than many of the people in those local churches.

"Some years ago," John continues, "I had lunch with a brand-new attorney who had just begun to work for one of the leading law firms in Fort Lauderdale. He came to know the Lord in high school and was trained in Youth EE. Still today he is leading people to Christ.

"In the near future there will be an explosion of youth pastors across this nation who will want to be trained in the principles and the methods of EE. This is one of the most exciting ministries that I could consider being a part of!"

In 1995 Rev. Rick Bond was appointed Vice President for Youth EE, the first full-time staff person to serve in that position. At that time, Rick estimates, about 60 churches were using Youth EE in the U.S. In six years that number has grown to about 450. In the years that Rick has been at the helm of Youth EE, 41 clinics have been conducted across America.

In 1996 Rick established the first EE Youth Advisory Council. Rick also set himself energetically to revise the Youth EE materials. Two levels of training materials and a beautiful youth version of the "Do You Know for Sure?" tract have now been published. Rick also has prepared an attractive Youth EE clinic administration manual and produces a Youth EE newsletter that enjoys a wide circulation.

The beneficiaries of this output stretch worldwide. The Youth EE materials have been translated into Spanish, Afrikaans, Bahasi (an Indonesian dialect), Romanian, Korean, Filipino, German and Taiwanese, as well as a cultural adaptation for use in Australia.

Interestingly, Rick at one time had serious reservations about EE's effectiveness with youth. But that has completely changed.

"Youth EE deepens a young person's commitment to evangelize," says Rick, "I had been in youth ministry for 18 years and figured I saw everything there was to see." But after Rick himself became equipped in EE, and while equipping his young people, he realized the impact EE could have on youth.

"I saw firsthand, a boldness and confidence and assurance of faith that I hadn't seen before in my young people," says Rick. "When it came to understanding and articulating their faith, I've never had teenagers come close to this."

While Youth EE equips young people to share their faith, it also has residual effects. "EE doesn't specifically teach about the peer pressures of life," Rick observes. "But we find that in EE, teens become more and more aware of their own lifestyle, and the fact that they can't be out sharing their faith while living a lifestyle inconsistent with what Christ would have them do."

Rick asks, "How many Christian adults have gone through their entire lives without sharing Christ with someone? Youth EE has teenagers sharing the Gospel, in many cases, almost every week."

Shayne Wheeler, Youth Pastor at New Life in Christ

Church in Fredericksburg, Virginia, testifies, "In the Spring of 1998 one of our pastors encouraged me and one of our interns to attend a youth clinic. Leery of 'canned' presentations of the Gospel, I was very hesitant to attend the clinic, much less implement it in our church's Youth Ministry.

"Through the testimonies of the teenagers at the clinic, however, I began to see it was not a 'canned' presentation.

"As the week went on, I saw teenagers leading other teenagers to Christ. It blew me away! At one point, as multiple 'lion and bear' stories were being shared, I raised my hand and asked, 'Are you guys making this up?' It was foreign to my experience to hear of so many people coming to faith in Christ in such extraordinary ways!

"The last evening our team went to a mall and it was my turn to share. It would be my first time to go through the entire EE outline and I was still cynical. To my surprise, the young man with whom I shared the Gospel prayed to receive Christ as his Savior, right there in the middle of the mall!

"I left the clinic fully confident in what the Lord could do through EE. I was eager to get home and begin to implement the training in our church. We began the first semester with nine of us meeting every Monday evening. In the first semester, our group was able to share the Gospel a total of 27 times with more than 30 people, five of them prayed to receive Christ as Savior!

"Youth EE invigorated the adults of our church. That same semester, we also saw six adults come to faith through Adult EE.

"We now have nine people who are able to train their friends on how to share Christ. Next semester we will have space for 27 people to be involved in Youth EE and there is a waiting list! Teens are lining up to take EE because they have seen the fruit.

The spiritual growth we have seen in our Youth Ministry has exceeded all my expectations. As we look forward to going to Romania with Youth EE next summer, we are truly on our way to being a Youth Ministry that reaches around the world."

Speaking of youth "reaching around the world," that's exactly what Youth EE has begun to do through its summer mission trips. In the past 15 years they have ministered in South Africa, Australia, Zimbabwe, Fiji, Swaziland, and 55 other nations!

These teenagers give up the opportunity to kick back, relax and mellow out from a tough year of school for an EE training manual. They give up Big Macs and fries for anchovies and *balut* (partially developed chick embryos). Their stomachs may never be the same, but neither will their hearts! They have been doing their part to change the world.

Kids' EE

Newly developed Kids' EE is winning children to Jesus Christ and teaching them how to lead others to Christ. It works!

"I was in Adult EE for years," says Anne Bailey, after beginning Kid's EE in her Warsaw, Indiana, church. "This is what I always wanted to do with children. This is the most exciting thing I've seen for kids in years, and I've worked in children's ministries for 30 years."

Anne Bailey's enthusiastic comment is typical. People are finding that Kids' EE is as effective in teaching kids to share the Gospel as its older brother, Youth EE. That's because Kids' EE is a visual, interactive approach that uses an age-appropriate curriculum that children can easily grasp. They can soak it up and wring it out as future life-style evangelists.

The Gospel Is for Everyone

Starting with the five "bare bones" points of the Gospel Outline, kids learn the key concepts, Scriptures and illustrations for each. This deepens their understanding of the "Good News" of the Gospel. And stories, object lessons, and hands-on experiences help youngsters take their "childhood" faith to a more mature level.

Since many kids aren't ready to listen to lectures and take notes, Kids' EE uses the four learning styles appropriate for children: auditory (hearing), visual (pictures), tactile (touch) and kinesthetic (motions). Kids' EE incorporates all four into a fun, interactive, fulfilling learning experience. Kids' EE materials are bright and attractive. The hands-on objects used to reinforce the concepts of each lesson capture kids' interest. Skits, cadences, and activities with movement engage children and make learning fun.

Kids' EE seeks to clarify the Gospel for children so they can come to true saving faith in Christ. They also develop confidence in sharing the Gospel with family members and friends.

Adults trained at Kids' EE clinics learn Kids' EE by experiencing it. They participate in everything the kids do: games, skits, motions. The teaching techniques are clearly different from those used with adults. But clinicians returning home and implementing Kids' EE soon see how effective it is in training kids to share their faith.

Kids' EE was launched in January 1999 under the guidance of Rick Bond. The pilot program was at Coral Ridge Presbyterian Church with Director of Children's Ministries Susie Miller, Knox Seminary Professor Dr. Sam Lamerson and Kids' EE Creative Specialist Pat Cannon working with a group of children in grades four to six.

On April 1, 2000, Dr. Karen Gushta assumed the position of full-time Director of Kids' EE. Karen had been a professor of teacher education at Nova Southeastern University in Ft. Lauderdale, but she felt called to engage in Christian education. With the urging of Susie Miller, she accepted the appointment as Director and brought her love for teaching children and training teachers to the position.

Karen took the initial training manual and spent hours and days refining it into an excellent tool for use in leadership clinics and local church training ministries. She and her husband, Richard, have been greatly used to promote the Kids' EE ministry among interested churches.

The first Kids' EE clinic was held in April 1999 at Coral Ridge Church with 15 people attending. Since the first clinic, a total of eight Kids' EE clinics have been held in the United States. The initial response to Kids' EE among churches and pastors is one of great excitement. These leaders know the importance of training children to share their faith, for children have a whole lifetime to do so. Many, therefore, are eager to get the training underway.

The reports about children who have been trained in Kids' EE are encouraging.

Allison is one example. Trained in Kids' EE as a 5th grader, Allison, now 13, has been sharing the Gospel with her friends and other kids. While still in 5th grade, she shared the Gospel with a friend at a slumber party. Allison's friend, who was from a Mormon background, prayed to receive the gift of eternal life through Jesus Christ.

Now that Allison is in Junior High, she is continuing to use her Kids' EE training. In January 2001 she started a Christian club at her school and it grew from 10 to 60. Allison invited youth pastors and other guest speakers to visit the club during its noontime meetings. When there was no guest speaker, Allison would share the Gospel with the kids, as she had learned to

The Gospel Is for Everyone

do in Kids' EE. By the end of the year at least 30 junior high kids had prayed to receive Christ. This year the club has continued with 60 kids regularly attending.

The adults involved in Kids' EE are also greatly impacted. Tamara White, from Moody Church, Chicago, attended a Kids' EE Clinic in October 2000 along with the Children's Ministry Director and two other children's ministry workers from the church. As the clinic came to a close, Tamara had to leave early. In her final oral presentation she stumbled and was unsure. She didn't appear to be the most promising of Kids' EE clinicians.

However, word soon came that Tamara and the three others from Moody Church were putting their training to use. Moody Church Sunday school teachers were being trained to use Kids' EE materials. And on the playgrounds of Cabrini Green, a large subsidized housing project near the church, these witnesses were using the two diagnostic questions to find out if children had received Christ's gift of eternal life. They were sharing the Gospel using Kids' EE teaching cards. As a result, the children now understood that "heaven is a free gift," and many were praying to receive eternal life through faith in Jesus Christ.

Due primarily to Tamara's efforts, Moody Church will serve as a clinic base for a Kids' EE Clinic in June 2002. The clinic at Moody Church will be among the six clinics to be held nationwide in the U.S. in 2002. As a volunteer who pays her own travel and ministry expenses, Tamara is making a great impact for Kids' EE and for God!

Haiti has been another success story for Kids' EE. Don Warren, EE Area Representative, and his wife, Suzy, have taught several Kids' EE clinics there. The clinicians have responded with great enthusiasm. In each clinic over 90 children have heard the Gospel. The majority of them have prayed to receive Christ as Savior.

Since its beginning in 1999, Kids' EE has quickly traveled overseas and is now fully established in the Philippines, Indonesia and Oceania. In 2002 it will be introduced in parts of Africa, India, Romania, Singapore and Ukraine. Materials are being translated into Afrikaans, Arabic, Finnish, French, German, Hindi, Russian, Spanish and Taiwanese.

It is increasingly evident that kids, too, can have a part in winning the world to Christ!

Seniors' EE

An anxious young woman called our office from Harrisburg, Pennsylvania. Could someone visit her 88-year-old grandfather, Bill? Bill had suffered a stroke and was in a Ft. Lauderdale nursing home, not expected to live. Bill was not a Christian.

Two women from our office, Beverly Wallhoff and Robbin Bernhhardt, both involved in our Seniors' EE, responded to the call. Before they left, the two prayed that Bill would be able to understand the Gospel and that the Holy Spirit would prepare his heart to receive Christ.

When Bev and Robbin arrived at the nursing home and found Bill, they let him know that his granddaughter had asked them to visit. They soon discovered that Bill was angry with God. Bill couldn't understand why a loving God would allow bad things to happen to good people. Without attempting to debate the issue, the two shared the Gospel. Despite his anger, he clung to every word. He was eager to understand the Bible and was pleased that someone had come to explain it to him in a way he could understand. He was glad to discover that he could go to heaven by placing his trust in the Lord Jesus Christ.

"Bill, would you like to ask Jesus to enter your life and for-

The Gospel Is for Everyone

give your sins?" one of the women inquired.

"I would be stupid not to ask Jesus into my heart," Bill replied. As Bev led him, he prayed to accept Jesus.

Only a few days later, Bill went to his heavenly home to meet his newly found Savior, and Bill's granddaughter has the assurance that she will see him again one day. What if two faithful women had not visited Bill and led him to Christ?

Visiting a nursing home, you will notice something very unusual. Many of the residents in wheelchairs position themselves at the doorways of their rooms. They're not seeking fresh air or a better view. From that spot they are looking down the usually vacant corridors, hoping someone will walk by they can talk to.

For most of them, it's a futile hope. The National Institute of Aging tells us that 60 percent of nursing home residents never have a visitor. Worse yet, EE teams have discovered that close to 90 percent are not saved. They are forgotten. They are lost, and few Christians are sharing with them the Good News of Jesus Christ.

That is changing! EE's new Seniors' EE is helping churches across America fulfill EE's stated vision to take the Good News to every age group. The stated purpose of Seniors' EE is to equip local churches to visit those who are confined by age or illness, and minister to them through prayer, friendship, evangelism and discipleship.

We have discovered in nursing homes a wide door of opportunity. First, residents there are desperately looking for fellowship. Second, many of them are at death's door and yearn to know the way to heaven. Third, unlike most of us who are always "on the run," they aren't going anywhere. They are "a captive audience!"

Seniors' EE started when a vibrant, enthusiastic lady named

Susan Ivey literally bounced into my office at EE. All aglow, she shouted, "It works! EE works in nursing homes!" Then, in rapid fire, she described to me how she had been visiting regularly in various extended care centers, sharing the Gospel and leading elderly people to Christ.

"Even Jewish people are open to the Gospel," she concluded.

My executive secretary, Beverly Wallhoff, came in to see what all the excitement was about and ended up asking if she could go visiting with Susan. As weeks of visitation turned into months, I asked Bev to take notes of what she was learning. I wanted her to help me put together a manual to assist EE trained people in ministering to this age group.

A Christian Foundation heard about it and gave us a generous grant to pay a director's salary for one year, but we didn't have anyone on the horizon to serve in that position. No one, that is, until Don Lutzmann, a faithful volunteer at our office, met Robbin Bernhardt. Robbin was a loan officer at the bank located in his retirement community. In conversation, he learned that Robbin was a lay EE teacher/trainer, had a passion for evangelism and loved elderly people.

Don called my office to recommend that she be brought on staff as Seniors' EE Director. We appointed her to the position, with the understanding it was for only one year, unless the Lord provided another generous grant.

It was a perfect match. Every Wednesday morning she and Beverly ministered in local nursing homes, taking Coral Ridge EE trainees with them. Meanwhile, Robbin worked zealously preparing the manual to equip EE-trained people to adapt their presentation to the elderly.

But in a year the funds ran out, the foundation did not renew its grant, and Robbin's contract with us at EE expired. What would we do now? Since we had no funds for Seniors'

EE, we started praying zealously that God would send us a retired couple who were financially independent, that is, who would require no salary. As usual, God far exceeds all we can ask or think.

Larry Piedt, the Northwest Airlines pilot who led the EE ministry at Bellevue Baptist for several years (mentioned in Chapter Two), called me at my office. He told me he had just moved into the area. He said that he and his wife Nancy had just become members at Coral Ridge Church. They were financially independent, and they wanted to serve EE in any way possible. What an amazing provision!

On January 1, 2002, Larry, who is also a lay clinic teacher, began serving as our new director of Seniors' EE. Isn't God good?

With ten days free from flying every month, Larry is initially putting the finishing touches on our Seniors' EE training manual. Hopefully, he and Nancy can then begin training a group of EE people here in South Florida. In time, they will share the ministry at various Advanced Seminars and Workshops across America.

Prison EE

During Terry's last four years in prison, he participated in EE, trained 20 inmates to share their faith and led many others to Christ. Upon his release from prison, Terry started his own business installing swimming pools. He also became involved in a local church. After his three years of probation, Terry went to an EE clinic with his former prison chaplain. Today, he is stepping out in faith to serve Christ full-time in EE Prison ministry.

Hundreds like Terry, through EE's witness and training, are experiencing the same emancipation and fulfillment in Christ.

One prison in Tennessee has been dramatically impacted by our Prison EE ministry. Four hundred of the 1,000 inmates have come to faith in Christ! Some of them now serve as EE teacher/trainers and many more as trainers.

The chaplain of that prison now requires any volunteers wanting to minister in his prison to take EE! Imagine converted, EE-trained prison inmates teaching and training pastors and lay people the biblical method of witnessing and training others! Prison EE is changing thousands of prisoners into useful servants of God.

Prison EE's first Director was T.J. Murvin, a retired United 747 airline pilot who was trained in EE at Coral Ridge Church by a very zealous EE trainer, Charlie Hainline.

Charlie had his own "shady business" (as he termed it), selling awnings for windows. The business helped him pay expenses and freed him for his favorite occupation—winning people to Christ. Three times every week he served as a trainer in EE. One night a week he taught EE at another church. And seven days a week he witnessed in local prisons.

Charlie set goals for the number of people he aimed to win each year. Each year he increased his goal by a hundred. Toward the end of his life, he was leading as many as 2,200 people annually, mostly prison inmates, to Christ. When Charlie could no longer walk, his trainees pushed his wheelchair into the prison wards (and even carried it and Charlie up apartment stairs).

But Charlie, for whatever reason, did not train his converts in the prisons. So when T.J. Murvin became EE's Director of Prison Ministries, he determined not only to win prisoners to Christ, but to teach them to win fellow prisoners. Every week, T.J. would go into Morgan County Regional Correction Facility near his home in Tennessee with four of his trainees.

The Gospel Is for Everyone

There they would hold EE training classes and witness.

On one such visit, T.J. and his men approached five prisoners in the midst of a card game.

"Mind if we interrupt your game?" T.J. asked, fully expecting a rebuff.

"Not at all!" one of the men replied. "What can we do for you?"

So T.J. explained that the chaplain's office was doing a questionnaire to find out about prisoners "and what they face." Before the session ended, all five men had trusted Christ as their Savior!

Until recently, most Christians working in prison ministry assumed that prisoners pay more attention to people from the outside. But experience is proving the opposite.

Inmates are far more interested in what their fellow inmates say. That is why EE has refocused its prison ministry to train converted inmates to reach their fellow prisoners for Christ.

For example, at Bushy Mountain Prison in Tennessee, a trainee inmate, Harry Jones, in his tenth week of EE training, shared the entire EE presentation. Two prisoners prayed with him to receive Jesus Christ as Savior and Lord. Meanwhile, in the next cell, EE trainee James Slagle shared the Gospel and two more inmates prayed the sinner's prayer. In that one semester of training, 110 inmates heard the Gospel and 69 made professions of faith!

There are more than 1.1 million people behind bars in America, and the most disturbing fact is that 80 percent of those released from prison will be back shortly. But there is much more positive news coming from Prison EE. Only 20 percent of the inmates who have received Christ into their lives while in prison will be repeat offenders.

There is another surprising fact: Prisoners are very open to the Gospel. That is why EE is so committed to equipping local church congregations to share their faith in prisons and to train inmates to do the same.

A few years ago T.J. Murvin, long past retirement age, stepped down from being Director. Rev. Arthur Hallett, involved in prison ministry since 1986, took over. He has done an able job of multiplying Prison EE. He has revised the Prison EE materials and is taking the prison ministry to a new level.

Based in Sarasota, Florida, Art started out training a few inmates in a local prison. In a year he had certified 100 students. Many of these were transferred to other institutions. Shortly thereafter, Art began getting calls from the prison chaplains, requesting EE at their facilities. As opportunity permitted, Art responded to prisons outside of Florida as well. Currently EE is ministering in more than 100 prisons across America.

Art has made it a practice to sponsor some of his top volunteers to EE clinics so they can assist him by teaching and overseeing EE at the prisons in their own areas. At present Art has seven such volunteers, four of whom are former inmates. Art has also met with Prison Fellowship leaders in Florida and looks forward to the day when Prison EE can be expanded into every prison and penitentiary in North America.

Intercultural EE

North America has become a melting pot of many cultures. The 2000 US census shows that 10.4 percent of the US population is foreign-born. Nineteen percent of American homes use a language other than English. In New York City, over 200 languages are spoken. In Houston, Texas, there are over 50 Chinese churches. The face of our communities has changed. It has become common to see more than one sign in front of a church, indicating the presence of a second congregation with services in another language.

While we are taking the EE ministry to every nation, we must not bypass those of other languages and cultures within our own borders. and culture. Thus, as EE was translated into the major world languages, we sensed we had the tools to equip pastors and lay leaders in our own country who speak those languages.

Instead of having to adapt English material to a different language and culture, we now have the ability to hold training sessions, and even clinics, in some of these very languages!

Woody Lajara, Vice President for Latin America, organized Hispanic clinics in several key cities. Buddy Gaines, while serving as Vice President for Asia, helped Chinese, Korean, Japanese and Filipino churches organize clinics. As a 20-year missionary in Vietnam, I was able to help translate EE into Vietnamese and assist able Vietnamese pastors in teaching a number of Vietnamese clinics.

In 1996, after Jack Hawthorne retired from serving in the Caribbean, I asked him to be a part-time Intercultural Ministries Director. Then in June 2000 God enabled us to give Intercultural Ministries a budget and a full-time director, Robert Foster, who had had 15 years of experience in cross-cultural ministry.

For the immediate future, EE's Intercultural Ministry has established the following aggressive goals:

- Within 18 months, identify 12 new intercultural churches that have the potential for becoming clinic bases
- Continue to work with 6 existing intercultural clinic churches to strengthen their ministries

- Conduct eight to ten intercultural EE training clinics in no less than six languages
- Train and certify at least 6 new intercultural clinic teachers and clinic leaders

It is clear that EE's Intercultural Ministry wants to do its part to change the world! May God be praised! And may He give the increase!

EE Canada

With the world's second largest land area (after Russia), our northern neighbor today is a mosaic of 18 million indigenous and immigrant people. Many of these people groups have retained much of their original culture. Although there is freedom of religion, Canada rapidly is becoming a secular state at every level of society.

EE was launched in Canada in October 1967. The Rev. Dr. Lindsay J. Howan, pastor of Riverside Baptist Church in Windsor, Ontario, and his Christian Education Director had attended a clinic in Ft. Lauderdale. There Dr. Howan had obtained from Jim Kennedy written permission to conduct a clinic and launch EE in Canada.

In 1970, a second clinic was hosted by Rev. John Moran at Parkway Bible Church in Scarborough, Ontario. Archie Parrish and Buddy Gaines were the teachers. In 1973, Dr. Berkley Reynolds attended a Ft. Lauderdale clinic and returned to begin EE at West Ellesmere United Church in Scarborough, Ontario, and to form an ad hoc Board of Directors. By 1978, EE was incorporated in Canada with Rev. Ed Carlson as its first director.

Ten years later the first French clinic was held in La Salle, Quebec. And in 1994 seven clinics were conducted across the country in French, Chinese, Tagalog (the official language of the Philippines) and English.

There was a brief decline in the mid-90s; then EE built up steadily under the zealous leadership of acting Executive Director Bill Hirons. Youth and Kids' EE are catching on quickly. There are clinic bases at churches in six provinces. Some forty churches across Canada actively promote EE.

We have traced the origins of Evangelism Explosion in Ft. Lauderdale, seen its development in North America and its spread around the globe. Now we shall take a closer look at the impact this ministry has had on the other world continents.

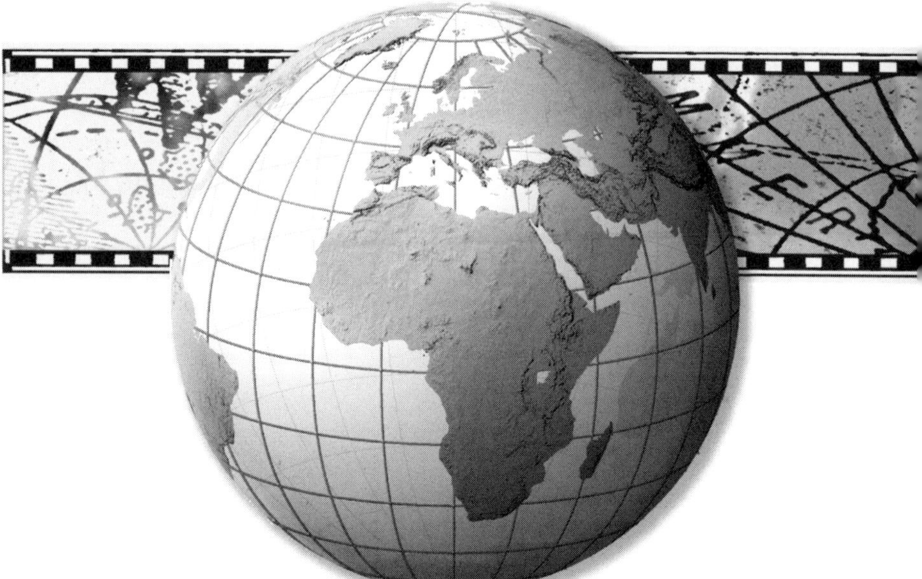

Europe
Rev. George Verzea
Vice President, Europe

*"They say people in Belgium are not open to the Gospel.
I use EE and EE works!"*
- Alex van Nes, Belgium

*"In a single night of on-the-job EE training, I saw
40 people trust Christ as their Savior."*
- David Parrish, Albania

Chapter 5

Europe: EE's Most Daunting Continent

FOR NEARLY HALF a century, the Iron Curtain divided Europe. Who could have anticipated the speed of its disintegration or the extensive religious freedom that followed? Unprecedented windows of Gospel opportunity are now open to the 530 million people who occupy this barely 4 percent of the world's land area.

Although religious freedom abounds throughout Europe, Evangelism Explosion has not had an easy time of it. Europe remains EE's most formidable challenge. More than on any other continent, difficulties have impeded the implementation of EE in Europe.

From North America, Evangelism Explosion first spread to Europe in 1975 through the indefatigable leadership of Archie Parrish. The ministry progressed through four stages of leadership—Vic Jakopson, a quintet of regional directors, Wade Weaver and George Verzea.

Each leader and the group of leaders impacted Europe in a significant way. To understand both the progress and the frustrations, we will look at EE's history in Europe from those four perspectives.

Vic Jakopson (1975-1987)

Britisher Vic Jakopson was trained at an EE Leadership Training Clinic in Fort Lauderdale, Florida. He was mentored by Executive Vice President Archie Parrish and returned to **Great Britain** to launch the ministry, with Archie, in Europe. That same year, 1975, the first seven-member Advisory Council was formed. In 1976 the first EE clinic, with 45 participants, was held at an Anglican Church in Northwood, Middlesex.

Under Vic's leadership, EE flourished. In a matter of 12 years an estimated 600 churches implemented the ministry. Many churches in Northern Ireland used EE. There was even a Northern Ireland EE Committee, which still exists, though not very actively. In fact, interest in EE throughout Great Britain has moderated sharply from what it was at the beginning. Nevertheless, several thousand people have been trained through EE since its inception.

EE's basic three levels of material were adapted and published for British use and translated into a number of European languages. EE Great Britain has been implemented in the four nations of England, Ireland, Scotland and Wales.

The financial support of Sir Cyril Black and the teaching of Archie Parrish contributed significantly to EE's initial success in Great Britain. The present director, Peter Crook, credits also the commitment of people like Pastor Bryan Alexander of Abertridwr, a small village just outside Caerphilly in South Wales. It is predominantly a working class community with a population of 3,500. The Abertridwr Community Church commenced its EE ministry in March 1983. Since then it has completed 19 local church semesters and held 10 Leadership Training Clinics. During this time 75 people have been trained in the local church and well over 200 have attended the Leadership Training Clinics. In 17 years the church at Abertridwr saw 600 percent growth. The large share of that was evangelistic growth, not transfer growth. It can be attributed directly to Evangelism Explosion.

Last year EE Great Britain was able to hold a clinic in Belfast. As a result, one church in Northern Ireland and two in the South are now using EE.

It was largely through Vic that Bernd Schlottoff, in 1976, introduced EE to Germany. The first EE clinic in **Germany** was held in 1980. Since then it has been followed by 20 others. Response to the training was good, but the leaders provided no on-the-job training. Without it and the hands-on experience it provided, many pastors failed to see the real value of EE and did not begin EE ministries in their churches.

In the year 2000, Reinhard Goseburg and a team of young leaders from Germany, Switzerland and Belgium restarted the EE ministry in those countries. They have translated new materials from the revised US 2000 version. The new materials were taught in two clinics, one in Germany and one in Austria. There are now three churches with EE training programs and the promise of many more in the future.

There is now a new, four-member Advisory Council for Germany, Switzerland and Austria. Leadership has passed from Bernd Schlottoff to Reinhard Goseberg.

With Vic Jakopson's encouragement, Oddvar Søvik trained the first pastors in **Denmark**, probably in 1977. The British version of the level one Training Notebook and the "Do You Know for Sure?" tract was translated into Danish. In 1980, the first clinic was held in Copenhagen with about 12 in attendance.

Explosion of Evangelism

Since then four more clinics have been held. Initial enthusiasm has waned. Only three churches have implemented an EE ministry. Conservative estimates put the number trained at about 100, and conversions through their witness at 150.

In the autumn of 1977, Oddvar Søvik, Martin Cave and Else Kari Bjerva from **Norway** attended an EE clinic in Southampton, England. Right after that, Oddvar introduced EE at the Inter Missions Bible School in Oslo. Several other Norwegians went over to England to be trained and EE training was started in Bergen, Oslo, and Stavanger.

Soon afterwards these workers and trainees formed a five-member Advisory Council with Ove Conrad Hanssen as chairman. The council made plans for the first Norwegian clinic, which was held in Stavanger in 1981. Some 20 people attended the clinic. EE had a fruitful decade (1981-1991) in Norway with two national clinics every year for a total of 22 clinics.

Initially, the response was good. Including a number of Bible school students, it is estimated that as many as 500 people completed the EE training. But the training materials proved ponderous for many lay people, who dropped out. However, almost every Bible school in Norway made EE training a part of the curriculum. Regrettably, since Oddvar Søvik, the Council's second chairman, left the board, EE has almost ceased in Norway.

But there is hope for its resurrection! Two years ago, Rev. Alf Kavli began EE in five Baptist churches around Lillehammer, central Norway. With God's hand upon the effort, EE may blossom again!

EE reached **France** through the efforts of Miriam Wheeler, who held a clinic in Paris in December, 1984. Eleven people took that first course. Later, Vic Jakopson came from Great Britain to help implement EE. In 1985, a five-member Advisory Council, chaired by Maurice Seauve, steered the EE ministry. Fifteen clinics have been held since the first one. The ministry grew well through 1995, then slackened off. In all, some 15 churches have implemented EE. Perhaps 220 people have been trained. All the basic EE materials have been translated into French and published. Moreover, EE France, through its published materials, has been instrumental in reaching Gabon; the Democratic Republic of Congo; French Switzerland; Belgium and Martinique.

In 1986, Vic Jakopson trained two church leaders in **Iceland**. The initial response was good, but only one pastor followed through with the training. He trained a total of eight people, who in turn led ten persons to Christ.

By 1987, Vic sensed very strongly that God was calling him into crusade evangelism. Accordingly, he resigned his position as Vice President for Europe and his EE duties were turned over to a steering committee.

Steering Committee (1987-1994)

On the Steering Committee, Rev. Malcolm Saunders represented the United Kingdom, France and Italy; Rev. Bernd Schlottoff, East and West Germany, Austria, Switzerland and Czechoslovakia; Dr. Theo Kunst, the Benelux countries; Rev. Oddvar Søvik, Scandinavia, Iceland and Israel; and Dr. Woody Lajara, Spain and Portugal.

Dr. Kunst introduced EE to **Belgium** at the Belgian Bible Institute. Later, Operation Mobilization used EE to do some training in local churches. But in those years no real EE clinic was held in Belgium. Therefore, we cannot talk about EE response in Belgium because EE was never begun in Belgium in an official and proper way.

Theo Kunst also introduced EE in **The Netherlands** around 1980. He taught the first clinic there a year or two later. The response was good, but, again, with no on-the-job training, EE's potential was not fulfilled. Growth of EE in Holland has been slow.

In 1982, Woody Lajara traveled to the Iberian Peninsula to introduce EE in **Spain, Portugal** and **Andorra**. Initially, Woody visited some key leaders he had known from previous years. They were very interested in the ministry and set up two meetings with other influential evangelical leaders. One meeting was in Madrid, the other in Lisbon.

As a result, EE provided scholarships to bring some of those key leaders to clinics in Tennessee, Florida, Arkansas and California. The following year, Woody Lajara and Ray Castro taught two clinics in Spain and one in Portugal. Together with the pastors returning from U.S. clinics, Woody organized an Advisory Council in each country which became responsible for the development of EE.

Still today Woody Lajara recalls a memorable anecdote from that era 20 years ago.

"When I visited some of the leaders in Madrid," Woody says, "a pastor told me very pointedly, 'This will never work in Spain.' He had 18 people in his congregation, and he wanted to see EE in action to prove that it *would not work* in the Spanish culture! So he and I visited some of the leaders in his small church. When I asked the two diagnostic questions, the pastor was surprised to discover these leaders were putting their trust in their own works, not in the work of Jesus Christ.

"Later, after the two men received Jesus as their personal Savior, the pastor said, 'Well, Woody, let's visit a professor of philosophy who has been at our church a couple of times and is interested in the evangelical movement. I have visited him sev-

Europe: EE's Most Daunting Continent

eral times, and we always end up discussing the philosophy of religion.'

"So the pastor and I visited the professor. After two hours, he, his wife and their two daughters accepted Jesus with tears in their eyes. The pastor was so excited about what he saw that in a couple of months we were teaching EE to the leadership of his church! Later on that church became a clinic base."

To date there have been 34 EE clinics in Spain and 24 in Portugal. Especially in Spain the response has been extremely positive. Some clinics have had to turn away applicants for want of room.

In Andorra, only one or two churches are involved in EE. In the whole Iberian Penninsula, some 30 churches have EE ministries that have trained to date as many as 4,000 people. These, in turn, have won an estimated 40,000 people to Christ.

Around 1990, Louis Simonfalvi, Arpad Revesz and D. Daniel Szabo, all from **Hungary,** were EE-trained in Great Britain. The first clinic was taught in Budapest in 1991 by Dr. Theo Kunst. Six seminary students attended. Since then some 20 clinics have been held, all with great interest.

A little Baptist Church on the south bank of Lake Balaton in Hungary, led by Andras Hegyi, has doubled its membership by using EE. EE has been taught in Reformed and Baptist seminaries. Hungary's Gypsies have also been reached through EE.

In 1990, Theo Kunst launched EE in **Romania.** Six Romanian Baptist pastors took the training at First Baptist Church in Fort Lauderdale. They returned to Romania and that fall started the EE ministry in their churches. How exciting that a land once totally closed to any evangelical work has suddenly become open to the Gospel! Indeed, Romania has become one of EE's most fertile fields.

One of the six pastors trained in Ft. Lauderdale, Vasile Talos, began an EE course that fall in his 500-member church. At the time, the church was having 70-100 visitors a Sunday, so the trainees had plenty of prospects to follow up. In 1991 Pastor Talos organized the first EE clinic in Romania with 14 attending. Since then, other churches have come aboard. EE leaders in Romania estimate that some 110 clinics have been held.

Conservative estimates put the number of people led to Christ through local church EE witness at 70,000. And, thanks largely to EE, Pastor Talos's church has given birth to 19 other congregations—a real growth explosion!

In 1992, George Verzea became EE National Director for Romania. In 1995, leaders set up a seven-member National Advisory Council. EE Romania has been instrumental also in introducing the ministry to **Moldova** and **Yugoslavia**.

Theo Kunst, about 1992, trained the first two pastors in **Slovakia** in EE methods. In 1996, the first clinic was held in Bratislava with 18 attending. Since then two more clinics have been held. The initial response was very positive. Forty people were trained in EE and 70 have come to Christ through EE.

Between 1987 and 1995 various pastors from **Finland** attended clinics in Europe and the U.S. In 1996, Pastor Petri Ruotsalainen attended a clinic in the U.S., led the first EE courses in the Baptist churches of Vaajakoski and Tampere, registered EE Finland and, with Tapio Sätilä, formed a four-member National Advisory Board in 1995. Interest among Finnish pastors is increasing. In the spring of 2001, Juha-Matti Hirvonen was appointed as Area Coordinator for Finland and the Baltics.

"EE has given Finland a significant tool to equip church members," Juha-Matti says. "In some churches it has restored evangelism to prominence. It has brought a life-changing experience to many pastors and church members."

Wade Weaver (1995-1997)

In 1995, Rev. Wade Weaver was appointed Vice President for Europe. He and his wife, Maria, had served for many years as missionaries in Spain. Now his EE ministry would be expanded to all of Europe. Wade was used of the Lord to lead EE's thrust into all the remaining nations of Europe **Greece, Albania, Liechtenstein, Malta, San Marino** and others.

In 1993, Wade had trained the first two pastors in **Croatia**. In 1995, he taught a clinic in **Lithuania**. The Lithuanian experience was memorable because two years earlier, Wade had encountered adamant opposition to EE on the part of some Lithuanian church leaders.

"I was surprised to find these leaders at the clinic," Wade recalls. "After the first day of training, it was clear that they had changed their minds about EE. By the end of the clinic, they were all convinced EE would help their churches. In three evenings of sharing the Gospel, 15 people came to Christ. One of the pastors asked how soon we could have another clinic. He felt that all the pastors in his nation needed to be trained."

Another breakthrough came in San Marino, where evangelism is illegal and no Protestant church exists. EE's way of presenting the Gospel in private is ideal for such situations. Wade befriended a San Marinan over coffee. Light talk led to serious talk and Wade led in with EE's two diagnostic questions, and the Gospel presentation, and a decision to receive Christ!

Leading someone to make a profession of faith is not the same as planting EE in a nation. In the fall, Wade and his wife, Maria, returned to San Marino to begin training his convert.

Alas! The man was unsure of his conversion. So for the next several months, Wade spent time, day after day, with his receptive friend. Around Christmas, the man recommitted his life to the Lord and agreed to be trained in EE methods. Now he is sharing his faith with others.

In 1997, Wade felt God calling him once again to pastoral ministry and resigned his post with EE. But he has not withdrawn from EE! He is actively leading his Witchita, Kansas, church in EE training.

When Wade resigned his responsibilities as Director for Europe, he recommended that EE appoint George Verzea, then Director of EE Romania, in his stead. George Verzea has turned out to be a wise choice!

George Verzea (1997-Present)

Vic Jakopson was the man who began the planting of EE in Europe, the Steering Committee continued the planting, and Wade Weaver completed it. George Verzea will be remembered as the leader who strengthened that planting. As God used Vic Jakopson and the Steering Committee to impact the Western and Northern nations of Europe, He has used Wade Weaver and George Verzea to impact Southern and Eastern Europe.

It was George Verzea who led the first EE clinic in **Albania**.

"I walked between two rows of soldiers into the small air terminal at Tirana," George says. "It was dark and foreboding, and I had been warned not to be out at night. In Albania there are only 7,000 Christians, mostly young people, in a population of 3 million. That first night I met two pastors who were anxious to be trained in EE.

"In Albania we have just one EE-trained pastor, Edmond Lemnica. Almost all the believers in his church are EE-trained so we had some trainers for our first clinic."

A few months later a group of 14 EE volunteers flew from the U.S. to help George with the clinic. Twenty-one Albanians attended. One was a pastor, his mind still traumatized by stories of rape, revenge and religious persecution. Another was Lindita, a former Muslim. She had been plagued by destructive eating and drinking habits and was filled with anger and bitterness. But God saved her and radically changed her. A third clinician, Linum, had violently opposed all forms of religion. When a fellow soldier in the Albanian army witnessed to him, he cursed God and slapped the soldier. Later Llirium felt guilty, apologized to the soldier and prayed to receive Christ as his Savior.

When the clinic leaders asked what EE was all about, a pastor spoke up: "EE is like a massive nuclear explosion spreading over Albania and the whole world!" During those few days in Tirana, the trainees shared the Gospel with more than a hundred people. Many prayed to receive Christ. David Parrish, who led the team from the States, declared, "Our lives will never be the same!"

In 1998, George wrote about his ministry in **Macedonia**: "There are only 350 believers in this nation of 2 million. While I was there, our EE leader, Venco Nakov, organized a clinic for three pastors. We field-tested the newly translated materials both in class and in visits to 11 of the trainees' friends, relatives and neighbors. Billiana, in the face of severe persecution from her family, trusted Christ.

"Our EE leader, Venco, also held an EE Awareness Seminar for 14 other pastors and church leaders. That's 90 percent of the church leaders in Macedonia!"

George Verzea has held other clinics in Hungary, Bulgaria, Yugoslavia, Slovenia, Greece, Italy, Bosnia. It's clear God raised

Explosion of Evangelism

up a multilingual Romanian like George to plant and build the EE ministry in Eastern Europe. He is also bringing Youth EE and Kids' EE to the continent.

George recognizes that in its desire to spread and grow, EE Europe faces some serious obstacles:

- In many places, EE classes have been taught without on-the-job training. This has seriously blighted EE's effectiveness. Many people claim EE does not work.
- Most churches in Europe prefer one-time evangelistic events rather than a discipleship ministry like EE, which requires time and hard work.
- Many churches in Western Europe, satisfied with short-term harvesting, have opted for a program called Alpha rather than EE.
- Evangelical churches in Southern and Eastern Europe are usually very small and very poor. They find it difficult to support a pastor, let alone EE field workers.
- Christian organizations in Southern and Eastern Europe are targeting the few available workers, hiring them for their own ministries.

Since taking over as Continental Vice President, George Verzea has instituted several ministry changes. These have reinvigorated EE ministry at a time when many naysayers were declaring that EE had outlived its usefulness, George has:

- Reestablished quality control of the EE ministry throughout the continent
- Refused to teach EE without on-the-job training—the proven key to its fruitfulness
- Replaced the old Steering Committee with a team of

young leaders committed to respect EE's core values and ministry non-negotiables
- Emphasized the importance of local church implementation, asking clinicians to submit in writing their projected "Implementation Plan"
- "Tabled" for a few years the appointment of Regional Directors in favor of Implementation Field Workers who are better positioned to reconstruct the ministry in each nation

Following the year 2000 European Leadership Conference held in Germany, George Verzea selected the following men to serve as Implementation Field Workers:

Juha-Matti Hirvonen . . . Finland and the Baltic Region
Samuel Mitrofan . . . . Southern Romania
Dan Măgureanu . . . . Youth ministry
Constantin Geamănu . . . . Western Romania
Daniel Lozneanu . . . . Eastern Romania
Alex van Nes . . . . Belgium
Liviu Mihet . . . . Northern Romania
Andreas Goseberg . . . . Germany
Eugeniusz Trczionkowsky . . . . Poland.
Helmut Kuhn . . . . Switzerland and Austria
Juan Diego . . . . Spain
Venco Nakov . . . . Macedonia and Bulgaria
Miguel Lilagostera . . . . Portugal
Drago Sukic . . . . Slovenia and Croatia

As he looks ahead ten years, George Verzea is believing God for mighty things. He would like to place at least one full-time implementation field worker in 31 European nations and

Explosion of Evangelism

have a clinic base in each. He would like to see top-quality EE materials translated into every European language and published. He would like EE to become self-supporting in every nation of Europe. And he would like for Evangelism Explosion to penetrate every evangelical denomination in Europe.

After a recent clinic in Slovenia, George wrote, "We discovered that God is working here, too. All the pastors in attendance asked us to help them implement EE in their churches. Some church leaders told me, 'Before the clinic, we only prayed, asking the Lord to send out workers into His harvest. Now we see that the Lord wants us to go!'

"I left Slovenia with great joy, because I found pastors and believers on fire for EE. During the clinic, I learned one important lesson: People are responsive to the Gospel. The Lord can bring revival to Europe. I saw God break down strongholds that have hindered the extension of His kingdom throughout Eastern Europe, and I think He can do it throughout all of Europe!"

Europe: EE's Most Daunting Continent

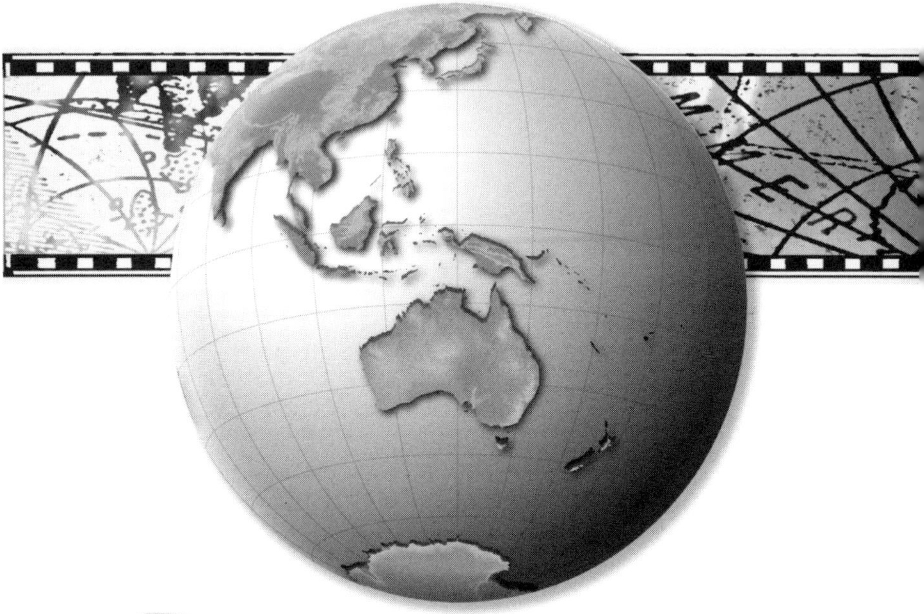

Oceania
Rev. Rod Story
Vice President, Oceania

"Since you introduced me to Jesus a year ago, I have read my Bible every day and worshipped at church every week."
- Hindu convert, Indonesia

"EE turns theory into practice, enabling ordinary people to share their faith effectively."
- An Australian pastor

Chapter 6

Wide, Wide Is Oceania

OCEANIA, SOMETIMES CALLED the South Pacific Basin, comprises 25 nations. They stretch from French Polynesia west to Indonesia and from the Northern Marianas south to New Zealand. It is an expanse of sea that spans 8,141 miles east-west and 4,736 miles north-south.

Oceania, by United Nations reckoning, includes Australia, the world's smallest continent, but sixth largest country, and New Zealand. It includes Indonesia, the world's largest archipelago, consisting of 13,677 islands. The region's religions run the gamut: Christianity of all varieties, Hinduism, Islam, Buddhism, animism and materialistic humanism.

Australia

EE was first introduced to Oceania in November 1975, when four Australians attended a clinic in Ft. Lauderdale, Florida. Rev. Dudly Foord, senior minister at St. Ives Anglican Church in Sydney; his wife Elizabeth; Church of Christ Minister Barry Cutchie; and Rev. Rod Story, youth pastor at an Anglican church in Brisbane, were the four participants.

Rod attended because his senior pastor, Rev. Harry Goodhew had met Dr. Kennedy in Laussanne, Switzerland, in 1974. He was impressed by what he had heard of the EE ministry.

The impact of the Ft. Lauderdale clinic on Rod was life-changing. "At the time, I had only begun full-time ministry as a youth pastor," Rod says. "I had a desire to see people come to Christ, but I lacked the tools to achieve my purpose. I returned to Australia strongly convinced of two realities. One, I could now lead people to the Lord. Two, I could equip others to do so, too."

In the first week after Rod returned home, he led three people to Christ. All three were 15-year-old members of the youth group in Brisbane. Later Rod trained the three in EE, and today, years later, they are effective leaders in that same church. Within the space of two years, Rod saw over 100 people come to Christ through the EE presentation.

"I was constantly seeing ordinary Christians transformed into effective communicators of the Gospel," Rod says. "And significant numbers of them developed the ability to equip others. That motivated me!"

In 1975, a year after the four returned from Ft. Lauderdale, EE was launched in the two churches. Within two years, clinics had been held in Sydney and Brisbane. EE was well on its way in Australia.

By 1980, interest in the ministry had increased to the point where it was time to consolidate the gains. Rod Story spent three months in Ft. Lauderdale, Florida, working with Rev. Archie Parrish and the EE international staff. He attended the clinics and received special training in coordinating an EE ministry.

At the end of 1980, Rod was appointed part-time Coordinator for EE ministry in Australia. In 1983 he became the first full-time National Director for Australia. Then, in 1987, while attending an International Leadership Conference in Ft. Lauderdale, Rod was invited to serve as Continental Vice President for Oceania.

In succeeding years Rod has invited leaders from other Oceania nations to attend EE's leadership clinics in Australia. From these prospective candidates, the EE ministry has been implemented throughout Oceania:

>   New Zealand 1984
>   Indonesia 1985
>   Vanuau 1989
>   Fiji 1989
>   Papua New Guinea 1989
>   Solomon Islands 1989
>   Cook Islands 1990
>   Northern Marianas 1990
>   Tonga 1991
>   Federated States of Micronesia 1991
>   Palau 1991
>   New Caledonia 1992
>   Marshall Islands 1992
>   Tuvalu 1993
>   Nauru 1994
>   Niue 1994
>   French Polynesia 1995

New Zealand

Good news travels fast "down under." And the good news can't get any better than the Good News of Jesus Christ and

His power to transform lives. Moreover, it wasn't long before New Zealanders were hearing about a Presbyterian church in Ft. Lauderdale, Florida, with impressive growth statistics. A Dr. D. James Kennedy had hit upon a method of equipping church members to witness. It was a method that *worked!* Kiwis are inveterate travelers. Some took the trip to Ft. Lauderdale to see for themselves.

Among them were two Anglican clergymen, Dick Tripp and Guy Nicholson. Upon their return to New Zealand, they immediately began training their church congregations. After that initial introduction of EE to New Zealand, other church leaders crossed the Tasman Sea to be trained in Sydney or Brisbane.

In 1984 five members of North Presbyterian Church, Invercargill, the southernmost city in New Zealand, attended a clinic led by Rod Story at St. Stephens Anglican Church in Cooparoo, Brisbane. They were impressed by the clarity of the Gospel presentations and people's responsiveness in the home visits. The sheer vitality of the host church amazed them. But like so many others, they pondered the question, "Will what works in Brisbane work in Invercargill?"

As it turned out, EE worked in Invercargill, too, and all over New Zealand! Two and a half years of equipping and witnessing added many new Christians to the North Presbyterian Church roll. Moreover, some long-standing church members came to personal active faith for the first time in their lives!

In 1987, the first EE Leadership Clinic in New Zealand was hosted by North Presbyterian Church. Twenty-two took the course, most of them from the South Island and most of them Presbyterians. A year later another clinic about the same size drew more people from the North Island.

In 1990 the first North Island clinic was held at Auckland.

Since then there have been clinics there every year, and these are spreading countrywide. In 1992 the first Advisory Committee was appointed.

By 1994 it was clear that volunteers could only carry the ministry so far. In 1995 Anne Bowie became the first half-time EE New Zealand Coordinator. In 1998 the position became full-time.

It was good news in New Zealand (and elsewhere) when Youth EE became available. EE workers were delighted to hear about the youth-friendly version of EE and to know that U.S. EE teams were prepared to train people in it. Carolyn Irvine, Youth Coordinator for Oceania, and Langdon Stewart, from Australia, have worked hard to get EE Youth established.

But of the EE variants, Kids' EE may be the fastest to gain ground in New Zealand. It had the advantage of good advance publicity. Pilot projects around the world demonstrated its effectiveness. In 2001 Virginia Woodward, newly appointed Kids' EE Director for Oceania, with assistance from her husband Dennis and her family, taught three Kids' EE clinics in New Zealand. Soon these new tools were being used in churches, after-school clubs, children's camps and a Christian school.

The impact of EE in New Zealand has gone deeper than a cursory look might suggest. In the past 28 years, hundreds of people have been trained to present the Gospel clearly, accurately and sensitively. They have done so within the context of friendship, and they have passed on this training to others. Many church leaders have proved its effectiveness in winning people to Christ and His church.

"There are hundreds of Christians all over this country who came to faith as a result of an EE presentation," says Coordinator Anne Bowie. "I'm constantly meeting them."

Certainly one of best things about EE is the confidence it

gives people to present the Christian faith. Laureen Tia, a New Zealander and one of the youngest Youth EE clinic teachers, reflected on this after her last clinic in early 2002.

"It's so exciting to see the transformation that takes place during a clinic," Laureen says. "People who were afraid to open their mouths to share their faith become confident to share it with anybody!"

Papua New Guinea

Papua New Guinea, just north of Australia, has some built-in problems. One is illiteracy. Another is the multiplicity of spoken languages. In a population of less than 5 million, there are 1,000 people groups speaking 862 languages! The community unit is the village, generally comprised of 50 to 300 people. In some areas, the villages are even smaller.

Papua New Guinea's challenge to EE resulted in still another EE variant: Village Evangelism Training. We condensed our normal EE Training Notebook so it could be adapted or used in churches with pre-literate and illiterate members. There is one advantage in such a culture: Because oral language is so important, people learn from memory extremely well.

The Rev. Sam Lowa, a pastor from Rabaul, attended a clinic in Sydney and returned to introduce the ministry to his area of Papua New Guinea. Over the years thousands of Papuans have been trained in EE. Currently Pastor Lowa is moderator of the United Church of Papua New Guinea. He serves also as chairman of the EE Papua New Guinea Board and is a member of the International Board of Evangelism Explosion.

Indonesia

Indonesia is a complex, diverse nation. Three hundred people groups speaking as many languages. Amid this diversity, there has been great civil unrest, as our newspapers have reported.

Much of the violence has been directed at Christians. In the past ten years, more than 1,000 churches have been burned to the ground—most in the last two years. Others have been reduced to mangled steel and rubble. Still-standing walls frequently are sprayed with graffiti demeaning Christianity.

Under this intense persecution, Indonesian Christians have remained faithful to Jesus Christ. "They tell us they don't know if they'll die tomorrow or not," says one visitor, "but they praise God because the persecution has strengthened their faith."

In 1993 a Java pastor wrote Rod Story to see if he would visit Indonesia. Rod did so and invited the pastor to attend an EE clinic in Australia. A missionary whom Rod met in Indonesia was skeptical. "I am sure EE works in America and Australia," the missionary conceded, "but it will not work in Indonesia."

After the clinic, the Indonesian pastor returned home to implemented EE in his church. Two years later, the first EE clinic was held in Java, using photocopies of the translated materials. The clinic spread EE to three or four other churches, and from there it spread to other parts of Indonesia. The growth was hard to sustain, owing to the diversity of the nation and its vastness.

Then a Christian and Missionary Alliance missionary, Rev. Tom Mangham, caught the vision and partnered with Rod Story to move EE forward. In 1999 the two, and others, developed a plan to train indigenous leaders to partner with clinic-trained pastors. These so-called Implementation Field Workers

Explosion of Evangelism

were carefully selected to contact all the pastors who had been trained in clinics in the previous three years. The result was significant development of EE across all of Indonesia.

Implementation rose dramatically from 20 percent to, in some cases, 95 percent or more.

A housewife trained in EE at her local church, led to Christ the maid who worked in her home, as well as a number of mothers of young children with whom she connected at school.

A university student, in the year following her EE training, shared the Gospel with over 200 university students, 179 of whom committed their lives to Christ. She is now working full-time with InterVarsity Fellowship.

A pastor, trained in the Bali clinic in 1998, now conducts two semesters of EE each year. During the first semester, his church added 50 members; during the second, 200 members!

A lecturer at a theological seminary in Indonesia shared the influence the training has had on him. Before EE, he would argue with people of other religions. Now he shares the Gospel gently and winsomely, leading many of them to Christ. To graduate from the seminary, each student is required to have two months of on-the-job training in EE.

A businessman testifies that for 20 years as a Christian he had never shared his faith or led someone to Christ. Now he does so regularly.

Not too long ago, Rod and I attended a gathering of over 850 EE trainers in Central Java. During the meeting we viewed an EE power-point presentation of the ministry in that area of Indonesia. Rod and I learned that during on-the-job training in local churches, 2,350 people heard the Gospel and 1,952 prayed to receive Christ! It was also reported that between January and August 2001 there had been 20 clinics training 856 clinicians, and 1,300 prayed to receive Christ. It was very exciting to hear the vision the people of that area have for the future of EE.

Micronesia

In 1988, Evelyn Palarca moved to Saipan in the Micronesian region, after attending an EE clinic in the Philippines. She was so excited by what she had learned that she encouraged the pastor of the Filipino fellowship in Saipan to allow her to use her training. As a result, a number of people in the fellowship were trained in EE .

Subsequently, Rev. Lito Rey and his wife Femie contacted the Oceania EE headquarters, asking that they themselves be more effectively trained. In 1990 Rod Story visited Saipan and led a clinic to train the first leaders in Micronesia. From this, the ministry spread across the Micronesian islands of Saipan and Guam. This resulted in the appointment of Robert del Rosario as Regional Director to stimulate EE across Micronesia.

Fiji

Evangelism Explosion in Fiji began with the attendance in April 1988 of the first Fijian pastors at a clinic in Wollongong, Australia. They returned to Fiji and implemented EE in 1989. They held a number of introductory seminars across the island. In August 1992 a layman, Bart Beatty, who had been EE-trained in Omaha, Nebraska, traveled to the Pacific and was challenged by the opportunities for developing personal evangelism. In 1994 Bart offered himself to assist in building the Oceania EE ministry and lived in Fiji for most of a year. Bart helped establish clinic bases, working alongside churches and assisting pastors in introducing EE.

In 1994 a Fijian pastor, Maikeli Ratu, began using EE in his local church. He motivated others to establish a strong EE ministry in Fiji. For a number of years, Maikeli has functioned as EE Coordinator for Fiji, and EE has been planted in hundreds of churches.

One Fijian church, Central Christian Center at Nausori, utilizing EE training, has grown in four years from 400 worshippers on Sunday morning to 800. Sixty-two cell groups have been formed by this church, and each of them uses EE to train its cell leaders. Over the past two years, 104 people have been trained in EE.

As a result of the EE ministry, Lautoka Gospel Tabernacle Church has grown from several hundred to upward of 4,000 people! In addition, the congregation has established 28 regional churches.

Mission Teams

A significant factor in developing the ministry across the Pacific and in harnessing the resources of the people trained has been the development of the mission team strategy. In 1987, a youth team from Coral Ridge Presbyterian Church visited Australia and introduced the Youth EE ministry. A team returned again in 1989. As a result of the impact of these two teams, Australia began to develop similar teams.

Figtree Church in Wollongong was one of these churches. Within four years, Figtree Church had more than 90 youth and young adults trained and participating in Pacific mission trips. All but 2 or 3 of the 90 have developed into strong, committed Christians, active in their local church. At least 10 are preparing for full-time ministry. Two are serving full- or part-time with EE.

Just since 1998, mission teams from Australia have planted

Youth EE in Indonesia, Vanuatu, Fiji, Tonga, Samoa, Papua New Guinea, Solomon Islands and Japan.

Last Territory

In chapter three you read that the island of Tokelau became the last *territory* in the world to be reached by Evangelism Explosion. Two years earlier, a number of Fijian EE trainers were equipped to serve as Implementation Field Workers. They committed themselves to short periods of full-time ministry with EE to assist local churches implement EE effectively.

One of them, Basil Hicks, traveled from Fiji to Samoa and developed a love for the people there. He also developed some connections with leaders in the small territory of Tokelau and volunteered to go to Tokelau to launch EE. Boats to and from Tokelau are infrequent. Basil had plenty of time—nearly two months—to train individual Christians to share their faith.

While there, he sensed God's call to a long-term EE commitment, so he has been appointed as Coordinator of the Samoan ministry. Christians in American Samoa have provided him with housing and he and his family will endeavor to establish a center for EE in that part of the Pacific.

Newest Nation

East Timor, after years of Indonesian rule and intervention by the United Nations, became an independent nation in 2001. Due to the massive bloodshed that preceded nationhood, the churches that had formerly cooperated with EE no longer were in existence. But since the formation of the new nation, EE has trained two leaders who are reintroducing EE into East Timor.

Australian Olympics

Running, throwing, shooting, rowing and witnessing! Oceania's Evangelism Explosion teams put on a gold medal feat during the two-week Olympic events last year in Sydney, Australia.

Two Sydney churches active in EE hosted three simultaneous EE clinics. More than 80 people were equipped during the six clinics. St. Matthew's Church in Manly, located by Sydney harbor in the center of the major Olympic tourist activities, opened an outdoor coffee shop which was staffed by EE teams. According to Rod Story, the coffee shop provided many opportunities for witnessing.

"Every team had positive experiences of dialoguing with people about the Christian faith," Rod Story says. "Numerous contacts were made for the host church, and it was very encouraging for new trainees, because they had some intensive opportunities to share the Gospel!"

On several occasions, buses of people from other churches came to assist. One group included a 70-year-old woman trained in EE. She exclaimed to Rod that it was her most rewarding spiritual experience ever! "She spent the entire day talking with people," says Rod, "and she presented the Gospel to more than 30 individuals, four of whom professed Christ as Savior."

Other church groups participated in drama, music, and testimony while a large screen displayed Olympic action. EE teams also had the opportunity to address personal needs. Rev. Richard Harvey of St. Matthew's tells of a man who stopped by the cafe. "He passed our church thousands of times, but had never come in," said Richard. "He saw the cafe in the church courtyard, sat down, and was soon in conversation with an EE team."

Wide, Wide Is Oceania

The man shared his story. It was not atypical: a broken marriage, depression, thoughts of suicide. In fact, at a drugstore just across the street from the church, he had just bought enough pills to kill himself. "I have no idea why I walked into this church courtyard," the man admitted.

Richard Harvey shared the Gospel with the man, who was unwilling to make an on-the-spot decision. But Richard arranged to meet him the next day, and on Sunday he attended church and professed Christ as Savior!

"I think he has some distance to go before he fully understands the Gospel," Richard says, "but he's well on his way!"

Youth EE in Oceania

Youth ministry is one of the most challenging opportunities in Oceania. Between mid-June and the end of July 2001, youth clinics were held in the Cook Islands, New Zealand, Vanuatu, Australia, Fiji and Papua New Guinea. In addition to the two teams from Australia, two other youth teams visited from the United States. About 400 youth pastors and leaders were equipped through those eight youth clinics.

In fact, one of the most significant developments over the past couple of years has been the raising up of staff to assist in the development of Youth EE ministries. In the year 2000 Carolyn Irvine was appointed Youth Coordinator for Oceania, the first continent anywhere in the world to have a youth coordinator. Carolyn is responsible for arranging and leading clinics, training clinic teachers and developing materials.

Kids' EE

In 2001 Mrs. Virginia Woodward offered to serve as a

Director of Kids' EE for Oceania. Virginia is a trained primary school teacher. Already she has launched Kids' EE in Australia, Vanuatu, New Zealand, Indonesia and Tonga. Virginia invited Don Warren, EE Director for Haiti, Jamaica and Belise, to visit Indonesia and help with one of the first Kids' EE clinics there.

Back home again, Don wrote:
"To say the least, it's humbling to be among brothers and sisters in the Lord who are suffering persecution. The people of Indonesia were encouraged and thankful when we introduced Kids' EE to them. 'Our kids are scared,' they told us, 'but you've given us a way to share with them the fact that this world isn't home. We're just pilgrims passing through here. Now they have the same peace we have.'"

Missionary visas for Indonesia are hard to get. Tracts are prohibited. EE on-the-job training must be done cautiously. Yet EE is being planted in the hearts of thousands of Indonesian kids who will carry on the work of evangelism. By God's grace, they will transform that island nation.

Rod Story and His Vision for EE Oceania

Rod Story is an amazing person! Several times I have been in his Australia home. I have preached in the church where he and his family worship and serve. I have traveled with Rod throughout Oceania. In every contact, Rod reflects the zeal and passion of a person who lives to fulfill Christ's Great Commission. Rod's wife, Rhonda, and the couple's two children, Tony and Anna, are also zealously involved in EE.

Although the church the family attends is a model of evangelism and missions, it was not always that way. Rod has inspired his pastor, his fellow members, and the church youth with Christ's mandate to reach their neighbors, to evangelize

Australia, and to take the Gospel of Jesus Christ to all of Oceania.

"My dream for the future," says Rod, "is to have the most relevant possible training for the individual cultures within Oceania. This includes:

- Internet-based training to make EE accessible to people in remote areas
- The most contemporary and user-friendly EE training possible for the local church
- High-quality, relevant discipleship and follow-up materials for villagers and islanders across the Pacific
- And a team of over 100 full- and part-time people called of God to strengthen and equip our Island churches"

Given enough time, and with God's blessing and empowering upon him, Rod Story may see that vision fulfilled!

Asia
Rev. Gary Letchworth
Vice President, Asia

"My vision is enlarged; my church is growing."
- Pastor in India

"I am reaching out (with EE) to customers in my beauty parlor, leading many of them to the Lord."
- Mary Wong, Bombay, India

Chapter 7

Asia: The Populous Continent

CONTINENTAL ASIA AND its immediate islands comprise 38 nations and 6 territories stretching from the Ural Mountains and Turkey to Japan. Asia accounts for a third of the world's land area. Its 4 billion people are three-fifths of the world's population. Asia boasts the world's tallest mountain (Mt. Everest at 29,028 feet) and the lowest land depression (the Dead Sea at 1,296 feet below sea level). Its "10-40 window"—a huge rectangle bounded by those longitudinal lines and stretching from the eastern shore of the Mediterranean through the Middle East, India, China and on to Japan—contains some of the world's most Gospel-resistant people.

From a humble beginning in Hong Kong in June 1977, the EE ministry has spread across the entire continent of Asia. By early 1996, it had reached every nation, and by 1999, every territory. Today, an estimated 125,000 Asians have been trained in EE, and through EE-trained people, more than 5 million have come to know Christ as their own personal Savior.

It began with Rev. E. H. ("Buddy") Gaines III, an OMS

missionary to Hong Kong. While on furlough in 1973, Buddy attended an EE clinic at Coral Ridge Presbyterian Church. Upon his return to Hong Kong, he introduced EE to me while I was serving as missionary pastor of the English-speaking congregation at Kowloon Tong Alliance Church.

Buddy helped me train others two nights a week. Largely through EE the church in three years grew from 60 to 360. The first EE clinic was held in March 1978 at Kowloon Tong Alliance Church with 63 clinicians in attendance. Rev. Archie Parrish was the teacher. Mr. (later Rev.) Young Man Chan interpreted for him.

Regional Directors

In August 1979, Buddy Gaines was appointed the first EE Continental Vice President for Asia. Under his excellent leadership, the ministry spread from Hong Kong to Taiwan, South Korea, Japan, Mongolia, mainland China, Macau, the Philippines, Malaysia, Singapore, Thailand, Burma, Indonesia, Laos, India, Pakistan, Israel, Egypt.

In August 1988, Rev. Gary Letchworth, was seconded to EE by World Witness to serve as West Asia Director under Buddy Gaines. During the next five years the EE ministry was planted in 16 West Asia nations. In January 1993, Buddy Gaines was promoted to International Vice President and Gary Letchworth became Vice President for Asia.

As the ministry grew and spread from nation to nation, it became apparent that Gary needed help with the administration of Asia. Wisely, he divided the continent into four regions: the Middle East, South Asia, Southeast Asia and Northeast Asia.

At the time, Rev. Milad Doss, an Egyptian by birth, was ministering to an Arabic-language congregation in Silver

Spring, Maryland. For 28 years he had searched for a good course in evangelism. When Gary Letchworth met him, he arranged for Milad to take EE training at Liberty Baptist Church in Hampton, Virginia. During his on-the-job training, Milad presented the Gospel to a Syrian woman living in Hampton. With tears of repentance she opened her heart to Jesus Christ. Milad was convinced that EE was just what he had been looking for!

Upon completing the course, Milad began translating the EE materials into Arabic, field-testing the translation on his Arabic congregation in Silver Spring. Milad and Gary traveled to several Middle East nations introducing EE to pastors whom Milad knew. It quickly became clear to Gary that Milad was God's chosen person to serve as EE's director for the Middle East.

Likewise, Gary found Tom Mangham under providential circumstances. Tom had been a missionary with The Christian and Missionary Alliance, serving for several years as Director of EE in Indonesia. When the Indonesian government refused to renew his resident visa, he and his family relocated to Penang, Malaysia, where his children were enrolled at Dalat School. Tom was a clear choice to be Regional Director for Southeast Asia. Gary traveled with Tom to several of the Southeast Asia nations to introduce him to EE leaders.

Buddy Gaines, likewise, was a natural to become EE's first Regional Director for Northeast Asia. It was he who had planted EE in Asia in the first place. At the time, Buddy was serving as Vice President for Eurasia and had mentored Dr. Nicholay Revtov as EE Eurasia's Director. This freed Buddy to take on additional responsibilities, so Gary approached Buddy with the idea of serving in both capacities—Vice President for Eurasia and Northeast Asia Director. It proved to be a perfect combination.

Explosion of Evangelism

That left only one region without a director—South Asia—which encompasses India and its surrounding neighbors. In 1995, Gary appointed Rev. Paul Devakumar, of Bangalore, India, as Regional Director for South Asia. Paul served until 1997, when he resigned to become full-time director of his own ministry. For a few years Gary felt comfortable overseeing that region. But in 1999, God raised up Tom Christenson and his wife, Fran, for the position. Tom had been a businessman with the gift of administration and a passion for witnessing. He and Fran had taken several ministry trips to India and felt called to serve there full-time.

Fran had just completed college, majoring in elementary education. She applied to do her practice teaching at the American Embassy School in India. When the embassy hired her, the India government gave Fran and Tom 10-year multiple-entry visas—something almost unheard of! Convinced that God had opened the door, Tom turned his business over to others, and in July, 1999, moved with Fran to Delhi, India.

At first, Gary appointed Tom as Coordinator of EE in India and traveled with Tom to various parts of India introducing him to EE leaders. After one year it became clear that Tom was God's chosen person for the position. So in the summer of 2000, Gary appointed Tom as South Asia Regional Director, and the Asia team was complete with four Regional Directors.

In the scope of this brief chapter it is impossible to tell how EE was planted and how it has developed in all 38 Asian nations. In some instances, it is not even prudent to report the progress, for it could put believers' lives in jeopardy. Enough to say that, by the grace of God, EE has made amazing progress. Reading these accounts that *can* be told should convince the most skeptical. We will take only a very limited glimpse at several nations or regions that represent the great work God has

Asia: The Populous Continent

done and is doing throughout Asia.

Taiwan

In 1980, two pastors from Taiwan went to the United States for EE clinic training. In March 1981, Buddy Gaines conducted three seminars in Taiwan for 130 pastors. He also spoke to 155 seminary students at Taiwan Theological College and met with professors of the Central Taiwan Theological College.

The first Taiwan EE clinic was held in February 1982 at the Tuh-Hsing Presbyterian Church. The pastor, Rev. Jung-Chi Lin, was one of the two men who had trained in Ft. Lauderdale. Since that first clinic, 59 other clinics have been conducted, preparing 1,223 teacher/trainers from 11 denominations. EE materials have been translated and published in both Mandarin and Taiwanese. For many years the EE ministry in Taiwan has been self-supporting and self-governing. It has its own Board of Directors and an office in Kaohsiung. The people of Taiwan, at their own expense, have exported EE to other nations, teaching EE clinics in neighboring nations.

In December 1985, EE Taiwan hosted the second EE Asian Leadership Conference, with 36 delegates from 11 nations (the first Leadership Conference was in HK in 1984, with 26 delegates). EE Taiwan also produces and markets the EE "??" lapel pins, both for themselves and other nations. The National Director, Elder Sheng-Hsiung Chuang, has been used mightily by God to coordinate EE in that nation.

The Philippines

Although EE Philippines dates its founding as 1984, its roots actually go back much farther. An American missionary,

Explosion of Evangelism

Rev. Charles Hufstetler, brought EE to the Philippines several years earlier. While on furlough in the early 1970s, he tried to attend an EE clinic, but found it was open only to pastors. However, he bought and studied all the available EE materials. Back again in the Philippines, Charles began his own EE training ministry. From it he saw abundant fruit.

The first official clinic was held in February 1982 at Kamuning Bible Christian Fellowship in Quezon City. From that first clinic, the number has grown to 259, and from that one local church doing EE, hundreds of churches now are implementing EE throughout the Philippines. EE currently is in 72 of the 73 Philippine provinces.

EE Philippines has an outstanding, fully supported Executive Director, Rev. Bernard Henson, an active Board of Trustees, 3 national and regional EE offices, 15 full-time staff and 30 volunteer clinic teachers The ministry is financially independent. All training materials have been translated into the three major dialects spoken in the Philippines. They are printed locally.

Back in January 1988, EE Philippines hosted, with the cooperation of 96 EE churches in Manila, an Asian Leaders' Conference. It concluded with a rally of 1,500 people involved or interested in EE. It was the largest EE gathering in Asia ever!

South Korea

In 1981, Rev. Man Poong Kim, Associate Pastor of the Nam Seoul Presbyterian Church, attended an EE clinic in Houston, Texas. He returned to Korea to translate EE materials and teach the lessons in his church.

In 1983, EE training began in Young-Dong Jungang Holiness Church. Participants approached the course with some skepticism. They agreed that EE was very systematic and logical. But would rank-and-file Koreans be willing to listen to such a long presentation of the Gospel? Was not the first diagnostic question too aggressive?

Once they got into the material, they found that EE was easily understood. Most of the pastors who received the training discovered new vision for their ministry. There were remarks like these: "Wonderful!" "Excellent!" "I'll certainly equip our church when I return home!" Others admitted they had been too busy ministering to do any witnessing. Said one, "During my 25 years in the pastorate, I've never shared the Gospel with anyone. Now I'll certainly make personal evangelism my life style."

To date, 127 EE clinics have been held in Korea, the largest in 1989 for 372 seminary students from ten different schools. Approximately 3,650 churches have been equipped in EE and some 71,640 people trained. In addition to the standard EE ministry, Koreans have adapted EE to minister to the disabled, to school teachers, to university students, to the military and to people living in fishing and agrarian villages.

Deaconess Chung-Suk Park is an example of the Korean's fervent love for lost people and their urgency to evangelize. As a housewife, she witnesses to taxi-drivers, store clerks, students on their way home from school and even to strangers sitting on a bench in the park. She personally leads about 450 people to Christ every year!

Japan

The development of EE in Japan has been more difficult. In 1983, Rev. Jiro Matsubara, with some missionaries from Japan, attended an EE Clinic in Hong Kong. Upon his return, he started translating the EE materials into Japanese and began training his church members. About that time, a group of six pastors and a missionary were invited to attend an EE Clinic in Dayton, Ohio.

The first advisory committee was formed in 1984. That same year the first EE Clinic was held in Rev. Matsubara's church with 21 clinicians. Since then there have been 14 other clinics. Several churches that initiated an EE ministry reported moderate success. Unfortunately, it did not last.

The Advisory Committee's chairman admits: "During the last three years we have not held any clinics because we were not able to register any clinicians." Since EE's inception, 30 churches have implemented EE, training about 150 people. About that same number have been led to faith in Christ. Please pray for Japan.

China

In October 1996, a quintet of mostly pastors conducted the first EE clinic at the Fu Qing Fu Hua Church in Fujian Province. Thirty clinicians attended. Since then, 35 other clinics have resulted in great church growth.

A report from Asia Director Buddy Gaines on two year-2000 clinics illustrates the responsiveness of the Chinese. One clinic was for "house church" participants, the other for members of the government-sanctioned "Three Self" churches. In the two clinics, a total of 82 teams went out for on-the-job training. The teams contacted 256 people. Of the 256 people, 176 listened to the Gospel presentation and 174 professed faith in Christ!

Just from those two clinics, 32 churches implemented EE ministry, training 1,380 people to witness. Those 1,380 reported 14,200 professions of faith!

During Buddy Gaines' September 2000 visit, China's first Advisory Board of 19 members was established. The next year, Rev. Mo Zhong An was appointed as first Director. Buddy reports that the Advisory Board has purchased property and plans to erect a six-story China EE headquarters building. Their ten-year goal is to take EE to all of China's 32 provinces.

But EE China is much more than numbers. It is people like movie actress Xuie Song (the name means "Snow Pine"). Beautiful, divorced and remarried, she had never been in a church. She did not own a Bible. But the indefatigable Buddy Gaines managed a luncheon appointment with her.

Buddy told me, "At lunch, my interpreter and I sat across the table from Xuie Song and shared with her the Gospel of Christ, using the EE conventional outline. She clung to the points of Grace, Man, God, Christ and Faith, and tears flooded her eyes.

"Did she want to receive the gift of eternal life? Yes! After we clarified the commitment, she prayed, repenting of her sins and placing her faith in Christ. When I asked her where she would awake if she passed away in her sleep, she replied, 'Heaven!' Then we shared with her the five next steps: Bible, Prayer, Worship, Fellowship and Witnessing.

"Xuie Song will be cared for with proper follow-up by a friend whom she did not know was a believer. She will attend church with that friend and make new friends. Yvonne will also visit her when back in Bejing. What a joy to see Snow Pine receive new life in Christ!"

Mongolia

In 1980, there was not one known Mongolian Christian anywhere in the world. Mongolia, with a population of 2.5 million people, was a nation spiritually dark—totally dark. But Mongolia is changing!

Buddy Gaines introduced EE to Mongolia in 1992, and Gary Letchworth taught the first clinic in 1993 at the Bible Institute started by Daniel Lam. Dash Dendev, one of the first eight Mongolian believers, was Gary's interpreter. Of the 23 clinicians who took the training, 17 were certified. During on-the-job training, 73 Mongolians heard the Gospel and 47 prayed to receive the gift of eternal life!

By 1998, there were Christian churches in Mongolia. That year, on another trip to Mongolia, Buddy met Pastor Badmaa of Faith Harvest Church in Ulaanbaatar, the capital. He introduced Pastor Badmaa to EE's main principles, and the next year he invited Pastor Badmaa and his wife to attend a clinic in the Philippines.

"It changed my life!" Pastor Badmaa says of the clinic. "I returned home and, using the two questions, shared the EE presentation widely and led 40 people to Christ!" Pastor Badmaa has translated the materials into Mongolian and used them to equip 7 others in his church. In September 2001, Faith Harvest Church held its first official EE Clinic, training 11 clinicians representing 8 Mongolian churches.

"Mongolian pastors want EE," Pastor Badmaa continues. "but until our clinic, they didn't know how EE works. Now, 8 churches are implementing EE. In August 2002, our church wants to host our second clinic. We are praying for 35 churches and 60 pastors and key lay people to attend. After that we will elect EE Mongolia's first Advisory Board."

Nepal

For many years, Nepal, located on India's northeast border,

was a "closed" nation. Hinduism was the sole religion of its 23 million people. Until 1950, there was not one known Nepali Christian anywhere in the world. But that is changing rapidly. Today, there are more than 750,000 Nepali believers, and churches are springing up all over the land.

In 1989, Gary Letchworth accompanied by William John, an Indian from Bombay, traveled to Nepal. While there, they visited several pastors, introducing them to EE. In 1990, Rev. Gopal Regmi was selected to attend an EE clinic in Singapore. After returning from the clinic, he worked with another translator to produce a Nepali version of the basic EE materials.

The first EE clinic was held in Katmandu in March 1993, taught by Gary Letchworth and Paul Devakumar. During the clinic 25 church leaders were trained and 52 people made professions of faith. A Hindu priest accepted Christ right in front of his temple!

At that time, Gopal Regmi pastored three small churches in the capital. In the following years he trained 2,600 people in EE and saw his 3 small churches grow to 40, with more than 4,000 believers.

Gopal has served as Coordinator of EE in Nepal since its beginning. Through EE, 220 churches have been equipped, and through those who were trained, 21 new people groups have been evangelized.

Witnessing in Nepal is not easy. EE trained believers have been ridiculed, imprisoned, beaten, stoned and driven from their villages. Near the Tibetan-Nepali border, one pastor bent on EE ministry found himself in a hail of stones thrown by an angry mob. Loyal friends hid him and he escaped, but he returned to the area again and again until people responded to the Gospel. Today there are at least four churches on that border—one with 20 believers trained in EE!

Middle East

Undoubtedly the most difficult nations in the world to evangelize are the Arabic-speaking, Muslim-dominated lands known as the Middle East. The history of EE there started with Gary Letchworth introducing EE to Milad and Margaret Doss. The two were trained at an EE clinic in 1989. After that, Milad translated the materials and Margaret typed his translation into a computer, using Arabic software.

For two years Milad Doss, as a volunteer, traveled with Gary planting EE in Arab countries. In 1993, Milad was appointed EE Director for the Middle East. Since then, through much blood, sweat and tears, Milad and Margaret have trained pastors and lay Christians throughout that area of the world.

In 1987, Pastor James Daniel, a Pakistani pastor, was EE-trained in Karachi. About that same time he was called to serve an Urdu congregation in Muscat, **Oman**. Immediately, he began training the members of his new congregation in EE, and soon had sufficient trainers to request an EE clinic. In 1991, two clinic teachers from Pakistan traveled to Oman and taught the first clinic there. In 1994, Rev. Alfred Samuel, the Egyptian pastor of the Arabic congregation in Oman, attended an EE clinic in Abu Dhabi and returned to train seven other people. It is estimated that over 500 Urdu and Arabic-speaking people have come to Christ through these EE-trained witnesses.

In 1991, the first two church leaders from **Jordan**, were provided scholarships to travel to the United States for EE training. In 1992, the first EE clinic was conducted in Amman with five leaders from **Iraq**, eight from **Syria** and four from Jordan attending. Since then, ten EE clinics have been conducted in Jordan, ten churches have implemented EE, 150 church leaders have been trained, and over 700 people have professed faith in Christ.

In 1992, five evangelical church leaders were trained in a clinic in Jordan and returned to Baghdad, Iraq. Rev. Karam Azab, an Egyptian pastor trained in EE, was called to lead their church. Together they launched EE in Baghdad. To date they have trained 110 of their church members and have seen church attendance grow from 400 to over 1000!

In 1992, eight pastors and church leaders from **Syria** attended an EE clinic in Amman, Jordan. Over the next several years, a total of 60 Syrian church leaders from 8 churches were trained in EE, and through their witness, an estimated 100 people have professed faith in Christ.

In 1993, the first EE clinic was held in **United Arab Emirates**. It was taught by Filipinos trained in EE. In 1995 the Egyptian pastor of the Arabic congregation of the International Church arranged for an EE clinic in Abu Dhabi. Pastors from all the Gulf countries gathered for the training, and in 1998 three more clinics were held. Now there are 32 Arabic-speaking believers trained in EE, and already they have led an estimated 50 people to Christ in a very anti-Christian sector of the world.

About 1984, two Scandinavian missionaries introduced EE in **Israel**. Although they held no clinics to train pastors and lay leaders, two churches using EE flourished as long as the missionaries were there. In 1994, the first EE clinic was held in Bethlehem, with only six people in attendance. A second clinic was held in 1996, this time with 32 pastors and church leaders present. At that time an Advisory Board was established and a volunteer coordinator appointed. In 1998 a third clinic was held in Nazareth, and clinics have continued every year since then. Most of the ministry has been to Palestinians. To date, over 75 have been trained in clinics and 165 Palestinians have been led

Explosion of Evangelism

to Christ.

In 1999 a clinic was held in Beirut, **Lebanon**, and a second one two years later. One at Mediterranean Bible College, the other at Baptist Seminary. In addition to these two schools, two churches are active in EE. Approximately 70 church leaders are equipped in EE and 110 people have been led to faith in Christ through the EE ministry.

In 2001, Milad and Margaret Doss went to **Bahrain** and held the first clinic for that island nation in the Persian Gulf. Since then the church has experienced great unity, 7 members have been trained in EE, and 30 people have come to Christ.

In 2002, a first-ever clinic is scheduled for **Kuwait**. Gary Letchworth and Milad Doss traveled there in 1992 to introduce EE to the only evangelical church in the country. Elder Emmanuel B. Ghareeb was sent to a clinic in Baltimore, Maryland, and returned to train five church leaders. As is the case in Muslim countries, most church members are expatriates who come and go, hence many members trained in EE return to their homelands. In 1995 a new pastor was EE-trained in Abu Dhabi, and now everything is in place for the church's first clinic!

The tragic terrorist events of September 11, 2001, have drawn the world's attention to the Middle East. Gary Letchworth reported recently that two former Muslim terrorists schooled in suicide attacks have been led to Christ by EE-trained believers in the Middle East. Both former terrorists have since been trained in EE clinics and one has led two other Muslims to Christ and brought them to an EE clinic. To the glory of God, EE is having a great impact upon the Middle East and upon all of Asia!

Asia is not only the largest continent in the world and the most populous, but in Asia EE is the most mature and indigenous. With God's blessing, EE hopes to win 2 million people

Asia: The Populous Continent

worldwide to Jesus Christ during 2002. In spite of the many areas of deep resistance, from the Islamic Middle East to Hindu India to Buddhist Southeast Asia to Shinto Japan, Asia could well see EE's largest share of those 2 million new followers of Jesus Christ.

We've looked briefly at God's formation process in the lives of Dr. D. James and Anne Lewis Kennedy. His divine work in their lives has made them the beloved leaders they are today. We've seen something of the trial-and-error struggle they both went through to bring Evangelism Explosion to the polished witnessing instrument it is today. We have traced EE's penetration of North America, its dogged efforts to gain a foothold throughout Europe, its spread across the island nations of the Pacific and its persistence to gain a hearing in every part of Asia.

Next we go to the continent that, more than any other, typifies "missions" to American churchgoers. But don't become too enamored with the stereotype! As you read on, you will likely be surprised by this EE perspective of Africa.

Africa
Dr. Ron Tyler
Vice President, Africa

"In EE we have a tool that can turn the tide of evil, stop the killing, and even bring great spiritual revival."
- Burundi pastor

"We are so happy EE is helping us reach our family and friends!"
- Muslim convert, Morocco

Chapter 8

Africa: The Hungry Continent

AFRICA IS BLESSED with great natural beauty, abundant wildlife, lush tropical vegetation, vibrant colors and warm-hearted, friendly people. Africa constitutes 20 percent of the world's land area (only 6 percent of it is arable), but a bare 10 percent of the world's population. Despite some industry and rich natural resources, Africa is essentially an agrarian continent.

A quarter of the world's nations are in Africa: 53 to be exact. The African pie, arbitrarily sliced by the colonizers of past centuries, gave scant attention to the 3,593 tribal divisions or the 1,995 languages and dialects they spoke. Much of the warfare that in recent decades has reduced whole nations to chaos can be traced to those arbitrary divisions. Possibly no other continent in the past 25 years has suffered such a series of political, economic, and natural disasters. Food production has actually declined as population increases.

It may be safely added that no other continent can match the *spiritual* hunger of Africa's people, and Evangelism Explosion is hard at work making the Bread of Life, Jesus Christ, available there.

EE was launched in South Africa in 1978. In the 1980's, EE leaders introduced the ministry in three other nations of southern Africa. In 1987, a missionary in Kenya started the ministry in the church he attended, making a total of five African nations in which EE was established. Starting in August 1988, the rapid expansion of EE began through the leadership of Dr. Ron Tyler. Ron is a Methodist missionary and was appointed the first EE Continental Vice President for Africa. Under Ron's leadership, the ministry was launched in 48 of the 53 African nations by the end of 1995. Today, as a result of EE, it is estimated that over 4 million Africans have come to know Christ as their personal Savior.

But I am getting ahead of the story.

In 1989, the first Kenya and Nigeria clinics were held. Also in 1989, two missionaries and two pastors from Gabon and the Democratic Republic of Congo (formerly Zaire) attended an EE Clinic in France. By the end of 1989, thirteen nations had started EE.

Then, in 1990 the Democratic Republic of Congo and Gabon held the first two Africa French clinics. Also, in 1990, Ghana and Uganda hosted their first clinics. By the end of 1990, EE had started in eighteen nations.

In 1991, the first Arabic North Africa clinic was held in Cairo, Egypt. The strategic clinic-base locations set up throughout the vast continent made it possible to expand EE more rapidly and more cost-effectively into the other nations. And spread it has.

Regional Directors

In the early 1990s, Ron asked faithful EE teacher/trainers

to help him reach into all the African nations and regions. These volunteer key leaders were Rev. Harold Peasley in Southern Africa, Dr. Dale Garside in Central Africa, Steve Ike in West Africa, Larry Walker in East Africa, and Rev. Milad Doss in North Africa. As the ministry expanded, these leaders were asked to give more time to help develop the ministry.

Eventually, the ministry called for Regional Directors for those same five regions: southern, central, west, east and north. At present, Twakkies du Toit (a former lawyer in South Africa) is the Southern Africa Regional Director; Chuck Baldwin (a former missionary pilot in Africa) is the Central Africa Regional Director; Steve Ike (a former accountant) is the West Africa Regional Director; Terry Jones (another former missionary pilot in Africa) is the East Africa Regional Director; and Rev. Milad Doss (an Egyptian and a pastor) serves as the North Africa Regional Director.

To tell you how EE developed in each of these African nations would require several books this size. Hence, we will take an admittedly brief glimpse, region by region, of a few of the nations. Hopefully, these accounts will represent the great work God has done *throughout* the continent.

Again, I must note that some nations, especially in North Africa, are very sensitive. To relate some of the exciting stories would jeopardize people's lives, even if I used fictitious names and altered the circumstances. In most of these North Africa nations Islam is a major religion that has hampered the planting and advancement of EE. Sufficient to say that in the past 23 years, EE, by the grace of God, has made amazing progress against this formidable opponent.

Since EE was launched in South Africa, we will begin with the region EE calls "Southern Africa."

Southern Africa

In 1978, Pastor Johan Landman launched Evangelism Explosion in Pretoria, South Africa, with a Leadership Training Clinic for 40 pastors and church leaders. Since then, 290 other clinics have been conducted in that nation. Those clinics equipped 5,320 more pastors and leaders. From the beginning, the response to EE was very positive. The ministry spread throughout South Africa to more than 100 denominations.

All the basic training materials have been translated and published in all 11 official languages of South Africa, making it possible for EE to train in any of those languages. A total of 940 churches has implemented EE, training more than 58,000 people.

The first Board of Directors was formed in 1979. In 1983, Rev. Harold Peasley, was appointed the first Director (later renamed Executive Director). The ministry grew rapidly through Harold's vision and efforts. He served a total of 17 years.

Early in its ministry, EE South Africa caught the Great Commission vision. It reached out to neighboring nations, taking clinics to Malawi, Zambia, Zimbabwe, Mozambique, Swaziland, Nambia, Botswana, Madagascar. It was even instrumental in taking EE to Thailand and Russia.

Twakkies du Toit, himself from South Africa and the current Regional Director for Southern Africa, presently encourages EE in 14 countries and territories. His vision and effort have helped build a strong foundation throughout the region.

Pastor Don Phillips and his wife, Nomsa, from Umtata Christian Church, attended a clinic in 1994. They returned to their church of about 150 members and began training others. Each week they held three EE classes, complete with on-the-job training. The church has grown to more than 4,000 members today, with more than 500 members EE trained.

Mr. Malcolm Thomas, who presently represents Africa as a member of the EE International Board, and his wife Linda are models of faithfulness. Since 1979, except for four semesters, they have taught two EE classes a year. To date they have trained more than 4,000 witnesses! Only God knows how much fruit there has been from their committed labors, as the seed sown has multiplied over 23 years, and they are still going strong!

In 1980, the Zimbabwe Methodist Church appointed Rev. Clifford Taylor to be its evangelism coordinator. After some research Clifford came across EE, liked it, and launched the ministry at Hillside Methodist Church in Bulawayo. In the first group he trained were Phil Whitehead, Phillip Laurence and Joan De Bee, Phil Whitehead's mother. As the ministry took root, the Methodist Church felt the need to train all their ministers. This demanded a clinic.

In 1981, the first clinic was held at Hillside Methodist Church, and attended by more than 37 pastors, including the then Methodist Church President and Pastor, Brian Anderson, from the Bulawayo Baptist Church. Many other clinics followed, with the help of EE teams from South Africa, led by Rev. Harold Peasley. EE became not simply the talk of the town, but the talk of the *nation*. Clinics spread quickly to Masvingo, Mutare, Harare and other cities. To date, 127 clinics have been held in Zimbabwe, and 2,037 pastors and lay leaders have been trained.

Central Africa

Missionary Jim Smith arrived in the Democratic Republic

of Congo, then known as Zaire, in 1978. One of his first steps was to establish a training school for pastors, evangelists, and Bible teachers. Because of his own experience with Evangelism Explosion in the States, Jim made EE the evangelism course for his school. In three months alone, his 45 EE-trained students had led 1,420 men and women to Christ!

Dr. Dale Garside and Pastor Dede Kikavuanga also had a large part in launching EE in the Democratic Republic of Congo. Their first of 20 clinics was held in Kinshasa, the capital. The response among pastors and churches was very enthusiastic. A healthy, steady growth has marked the advance ever since. In fact, DRC may have more EE trainers than any other country in French-speaking Africa.

Despite civil war, political upheaval and natural disasters, at least 25 churches are implementing EE. These churches have given on-the-job training to at least 1,500 people who, in turn, have led 15,000 people to Christ. DRC has its own five-member Advisory Board and its own director. All the basic EE training materials have been translated and published.

The DRC has also reached out to Angola, Benin, Cameroon, Cape Verde Islands, Republic of Congo, Côte d'Ivoire, Madagascar, Mauritius and São Tomé and Príncipe.

Dale Garside and Dede Kikavuanga made another important contribution to EE's growth and development. In 1990 they helped plant a church in an upper middle-class area of Kinshasa. That sector of the capital had no evangelical, or even Protestant, witness. Partly through EE, the church grew from 60 in 1991 to over 2,000 in the year 2000. The Church on the Rock, as it is called, has over 40 EE trainers going out on visits each week. It is a model church for many others in Kinshasa.

In 1994, Bishop Bahati returned to St. Peter's Church in Bukavu, after his training in EE at the International School of

Evangelism in Kinshasa. Before his EE training, he was quietly and faithfully serving his congregation. Now he was much more dynamic, zealously training the laity of his church, faithfully visiting and evangelizing. He planned for his church to host the first EE clinic in Eastern DRC. People wanted to know what had transformed him. It turned out to be not a "what" but a "Who." Through his EE training God had transformed his life.

Rather recently, the first French-language EE Clinic was held in Yaoundé. Twenty pastors came for training. The first evening the group "prayed through" the neighborhoods where the teams would be visiting. During the days of visitation, 73 people opened their hearts to receive Christ. One of those who gave her life to Christ also asked prayer for her daughter, who had not spoken in over four years. The next day the girl was speaking freely. Another woman was critically overdue in delivering her baby. She not only gave her heart to the Lord but that same evening gave birth to a healthy baby boy!

East Africa

In 1988, EE's newly appointed Vice President for Africa, Dr. Ron Tyler, moved with his wife Belinda and their two children to Nairobi, Kenya. There they set up a continental office from which Rod would direct EE ministry throughout Africa.

Not long after their arrival in Kenya, Ron traveled to Ghana, Liberia and Uganda, selecting key leaders to attend the first Kenya EE Clinic to be held at Good Shepherd Africa Gospel Church in Nairobi. Ron was assisted in the clinic by Larry Walker, the missionary who began EE in Kenya; Rev. John Muehleisen, the missionary pastor of Good Shepherd Church; and Allen Avery, a missionary living in Zimbabwe.

The 18 pastors and church leaders who attended the clinic

Explosion of Evangelism

were enthusiastic. Most of them returned home and established their own clinic bases. Thus EE spread. Currently some 200 churches in Kenya continue to provide EE training. Approximately 3,500 people have been trained to date, and they have led an estimated 20,000 men and women to Christ.

In 1993 an Advisory Council was set up which presently is being reorganized as a five-member Board of Directors. A fulltime paid director for Kenya was appointed in 1999. All of the basic training materials have been translated and published in English and Swahili. EE has reached 22 different people groups within Kenya and assisted Tanzania in organizing its own EE clinics. The first national office with its own staff in East Africa was set up in Nairobi, and that office has become the EE headquarters for all of East Africa.

After attending the 1989 EE Clinic held in Kenya, Pastor Gary Skinner and two of his associate pastors returned to Uganda to begin EE there. Because of its well-watered, fertile land and temperate climate, Uganda has been called the "pearl of Africa." But with the beauty has come great suffering. No one can accurately estimate the number of people who perished during Idi Amin's ruthless dictatorship and the subsequent civil wars, famines, and tribal killings. Estimates vary from 800,000 to 2,000,000. Uganda also has the highest known incidence of AIDS. An estimated 25-30 percent of the population has been infected.

The first Uganda EE Clinic was held in November, 1990. It was taught by Ron Tyler and Larry Walker at Kampala Pentecostal Church. As a direct result, the 2,000-member church grew five-fold to 10,000! In the past four years it has been reaching out to other churches in Uganda and seeing an impact there as well. Since the start of EE in Uganda, some 2,500 pastors and lay people have been trained, and upward of 15,000 people have been won to Christ.

West Africa

Christophe Dembele was first trained in a clinic in Yamoussoukro, Côte d'Ivoire (formerly known as Ivory Coast), in 1992. He returned to Mali and began training the leaders of his church in Bamako. Since being trained in EE and implementing it within his congregation, his church has been instrumental in starting five daughter churches. The first Mali EE clinic was conducted in June 1994 for 22 pastors and church leaders. Since then, 14 more clinics have been held in Mali.

Initially, pastors and churches in West Africa had a "wait and see" attitude toward EE. But the tremendous church growth associated with EE quickly convinced the skeptics, and the interest in EE among various denominations has been steady.

West Africa appointed its first director in 1994. The leadership of Christophe Dembele has been the most significant contribution to EE's success and growth. Christophe got off to a rough start. Three different groups of trainees quit on him! But he kept at it, and God honored his perseverance. The first Advisory Council was established in 1999 with four members.

The Clinic Notebook, Training Notebook, and various "Partner" booklets have been translated into Bambara, the mother tongue of most Malians. Leaders and pastors from neighboring nations (Senegal, Burkina Faso, and Niger) have been trained at Mali clinics. Currently, EE is training pastors who are working among a so-called unreached people group, the Bozo. Several mission groups have targeted this group, but for various reasons none were able to stay. Local pastors with a heart for these people are now being trained, and the walls of isolation are beginning to come down.

The first Togo clinic was to be held in Lome, the capital, on a specified Monday. Steve Ike, the West Africa Regional Director, arrived the Thursday before, ready to teach. But when he consulted with Pastor Afan, his Togo contact, there were problems. First, Pastor Afan had not received word concerning the clinic dates or of Steve Ike's coming, nor had the materials arrived from Côte d'Ivoire. Also, the Togo government was nine months behind in its payroll, and no one had money to pay the nominal clinic costs. It seemed like a formidable set of circumstances.

Steve sent out word to contacts in the United States, and godly people began to pray. One church offered to underwrite the training. But a clinic without training materials? Sunday morning Steve waited on the Lord for direction. He came upon 2 Timothy 2:2: "These things which you have heard from me . . . entrust to faithful men, who will be able to teach others also." *That is exactly what EE is all about!,* Steve thought. *God must want us to go ahead.*

Ten minutes before the clinic was to start on Monday morning, the materials arrived by bus, and the clinic opened with 15 registered trainees! As people prayed and gave, God turned an overwhelming challenge into reality!

North Africa

In 1990, Milad Doss, the Egyptian expatriate whom we met in previous chapters, traveled to Egypt to introduce EE to some of his fellow Egyptian pastors. Traveling with him was Gary Letchworth, also introduced in Chapter Seven. Both men had the blessing of Ron Tyler, Continental Vice President for Africa.

Africa: The Hungry Continent

In addition to introducing EE, Milad and Gary selected an Egyptian pastor, Karam Azab, to receive EE training at Coral Ridge Presbyterian Church in Ft. Lauderdale, Florida. The next February (1991), Karam, after receiving the EE training, returned to Cairo, where he equipped ten church leaders at his Shobra Evangelical Church. Milad and his wife Margaret taught the first EE clinic in the Shobra Church. The training materials, in Arabic, were photocopied for that first clinic.

That September, 1991, Inverness Presbyterian Church in Baltimore, Maryland, provided scholarships for two other Egyptian pastors to take the EE training in Baltimore. In 1995, a pastor from Alexandria, Egypt, was trained at Egypt's second clinic in Cairo. He has since equipped 21 church leaders in his church. In 1996, his church in Alexandria hosted its first clinic. In 1998, a pastor from Sohaj, Upper Egypt, was trained in a Cairo clinic. Gradually, EE was working its way through the admittedly small Christian community in Egypt.

Since EE Egypt's humble beginning barely a decade ago, thirteen clinics have been conducted, and 291 church leaders have been trained. Local churches have equipped over 800 men and women. During on-the-job training, over 2,000 Egyptians have been led to faith in Christ.

Milad Doss, incidentally, wears two EE hats. He serves under Gary Letchworth, Vice President, Asia, as EE's Middle East Regional Director, and he serves under Ron Tyler, Vice President, Africa, as EE's North Africa Regional Director. In all, he is responsible for ministry in 22 nations on two continents.

With the exception of a limited number of Christian churches in Egypt and the Anglican Church in Libya, all of North Africa is solidly Islamic. To be a citizen of Algeria, Libya, Mauritania, Morocco or Tunisia is to be a Muslim. But

Explosion of Evangelism

there *are* Christian believers in all of these nations. They worship clandestinely, meeting in secret fellowships. EE clinics are usually held in secret locations, moving from one place to another in the course of a week's training. Yet even at the peril of their lives, these EE-trained believers are often bold, witnessing with heroic zeal.

Beyond Africa

In 1994, missionaries in Ceuta, Spain, contacted Ron Tyler, requesting EE training for Moroccan believers. Ron recruited the faithful Milad and Margaret Doss for the job. They held the first EE clinic for Moroccans in Ceuta. Actually, only two believers showed up for the training. One was Moroccan, the other was a missionary serving in North Africa. During on-the-job training, the team led three people to Christ.

At the end of that year, 1994, while attending a conference for North Africa workers, Milad met a missionary living and working in Casablanca. That missionary requested that Milad teach EE to his contacts, which he did the following year. Hence, the first Casablanca EE clinic was conducted in secret. Twenty-four believers came, including two from Mauritania and one from Algeria.

In 1996, an Advisory Council was formed with a missionary serving as coordinator. In 2000, a national pastor accepted the position of EE Morocco coordinator. Since 1995, six clinics have been held in Morocco. Only one year went by without a clinic there. It is estimated that in all of Morocco, there are only 1,200 believers. Of those, 137 have been trained in EE, and their witness in turn has produced nearly 200 other professions of faith.

Africa: The Hungry Continent

Ron Tyler

Ron Tyler, EE's Vice President for Africa, is a man of faith and vision. Back in 1975, at a Christian retreat, he prayed, "Lord, I'll go anywhere you want me to go. I'll do anything you want me to do. I'll be anything you want me to be." At the time he was a senior programmer with a computer company in Atlanta, Georgia. But Ron felt God saying to him, "I plan to use you to reach hundreds of thousands of people for Christ."

For the next 13 years God prepared Ron for that very purpose. He went to seminary, held several pastorates, equipped his congregations in EE, took doctoral studies, and applied for missionary service. Then one day Dr. Woody Lajara, at that time EE's Executive Vice President, called Ron and asked him if he would consider being interviewed for the position of Vice President for Africa, responsible for introducing, developing, and overseeing the EE ministry throughout that continent.

"It was as if a light bulb went on!" Ron said. "This is it! This is how the Lord is going to accomplish what He told me in 1975!" Belinda and Ron were enjoying ministry in the local church. It was growing. They were in the middle of a building program. It was exciting what the Lord was doing. But Ron knew that God was preparing them both for a giant step of faith. In February 1988, the congregation moved into its new building, debt free.

"That March," Ron says, "I told my church that Belinda and I would be leaving them in June and moving to Nairobi, Kenya, in August. Many pastor friends told us we were crazy to leave the church when everything was going so well, but we believed the Lord was leading us.

"Before leaving for Africa, I asked Dr. Kennedy if he had any last minute instructions. He replied, 'Go start EE in every nation of Africa!'

"When we arrived in Nairobi, EE was in four southern African nations and in Kenya, East Africa. Forty-eight other nations had to be added! I had been challenged by Dr. Kennedy to complete the task by the end of 1995! I knew that was impossible for *me* to do. But December 28, 1995, with God's help, EE began in Libya, the last of the 53 Africa nations to launch EE!

"We now must organize the leadership structure in Africa. We must undergird what has been accomplished and let it serve as a launching pad for the next major challenge. And what is that next challenge? It is to reach each of the 3,593 African tribes speaking 1,995 different languages.

"To do this we will need visionary churches and businessmen in Africa and on other continents to support our effort with much prayer and money. We will need to add many more field workers who will use the 'FlipChart' training to reach those tribes and languages."

Ron tends to be modest about his FlipCharts, but they well could be the key to winning Africa to Jesus Christ.

"Several years ago," Ron explains, "I prayed, 'Lord, we can reach maybe 20-30 percent of Africans with our EE materials, but what about the rest of the people? Many can barely read or write. I know You love them also!'

"And the Lord seemed to say to me, 'Pictures! Use pictures to reach them.' The pressure to get into every African nation took precedence, but later I began putting the new material together. For lack of a name, I called it the EE FlipChart. It was a flip chart of pictures. We reviewed the EE Clinic and Training Notebooks, deciding what should be the bare minimum, without compromising EE standards and principles.

"When the material was finished, I let Agrippa Dube and

his staff field test it in Zimbabwe. It worked!

"When I explained the new approach to a Zimbabwe EE field worker, tears welled in his eyes and a giant smile covered his face. He explained, 'My father is a pastor, but he can barely read and write. I tried to teach him EE, using the current materials. He said it was too difficult to learn. But the FlipChart material will work! He can learn it!.' And the man's father did learn the EE presentation through the EE FlipChart.

"In two years," Ron went on to say, "more than 200 people were equipped in EE with this method. A woman from one village, with no formal education, learned the EE presentation taught by her pastor using the EE FlipChart. In her own home she led her husband and ten-year-old daughter to Christ.

"The woman's daughter has since also learned the EE presentation and is leading her friends to Christ. One villager exclaimed, 'Other groups have passed us by because we can't read or write. EE has done something no one else could do! Thank you for caring about us!'"

"Can we win all of Africa? Some people may declare it impossible. But with God, all things are possible. Through the Lord and His people, we will again see the impossible become a reality!"

One of the highlights of my life and ministry took place on a trip with Ron Tyler to the rocky southernmost tip of Africa. There, at Cape Good Hope, the two of us stood with a group of EE-trained brothers, praying. Above us was the towering lighthouse that guides sea captains around that treacherous point of land where the Indian Ocean meets the Atlantic. Behind us—indeed, under foot—was Africa, diverse and still needy despite more than two centuries of missionary endeavor.

As we prayed there together, all of us sensed that God was helping us in EE to fulfill what Isaiah had prophesied more

Explosion of Evangelism

than 26 centuries earlier:

> *"I will also make you a light for the Gentiles,
> that you may bring my salvation to the ends of the earth."*
>
> –Isaiah 49:6b (NIV)

Africa: The Hungry Continent

Latin America
Dr. Woody Lajara
Vice President, Latin America

"I have lost my fear to witness!"
- Venezuelan pastor

"Seminary never trained me how to witness. Thanks for training us!"
- A pastor in Mexico

Chapter 9

Latin America: The Explosion Has Been Dramatic

LATIN AMERICA IS where Evangelism Explosion *truly* flourishes. I personally saw some of this phenomenal growth when I visited a young church in Costa Rica. I greeted the pastor with the usual amenities. After a few minutes of small talk, the pastor became serious. He wanted me to convey a message to Dr. D. James Kennedy, EE's founder and president.

"Please tell Dr. Kennedy that he is causing a lot of problems down here!" the pastor said.

Of course, I was genuinely concerned. Part of my job is to resolve any problems that relate to EE. "What kind of problems?" I wanted to know.

The pastor explained. "Since we have been trained in EE," he said, "our storefront church grew so much we had to buy the store next door and knock down the dividing wall. We kept adding new believers until we had to buy a *third* store!"

"And why is that a problem?" I asked.

"Our EE teams continue to lead so many people to Christ that we now have to buy still *another* store. As yet, we cannot afford any more stores. *That's the problem!*" he said with a broad smile.

Dr. *"Woody" Lajara*

Why has Evangelism Explosion done so well in Latin America? Has the Latino temperament of so many of the people played a role? Have the vexing socio-economic conditions throughout the continent contributed? What about leadership both within EE and in the Latino churches? Answer: all of the above. But certainly the leadership of Continental Vice President Woody Lajara has been a telling factor in EE's success.

As Dr. Lajara himself has remarked on many occasions, "I have 'EE blood'!" Woody is a zealous, expert, ever-faithful witness. On two occasions he has suffered heart attacks that hospitalized him for several days, but that did not stop him from sharing the Gospel! While he was lying in a Puerto Rico hospital bed, many friends, relatives, and nurses visited his bedside. Before he checked out of the hospital, Woody, with the help of Will Rodriguez, his host in Puerto Rico, had led 27 of those visitors and nurses to faith in Jesus Christ!

On Woody Lajara's first visit to Nicaragua, the country was still under Communist rule. As Woody was going through the immigration line at the airport, a young officer saw from Woody's visa that he would be meeting with Christian pastors.

Communist law prohibited such meetings. Angry, the officer at first wanted to send Woody back to Miami. Instead, he made sure an officer was assigned to watch Woody 24 hours a day.

In Woody's Managua hotel room, the assigned Communist officer observing, Woody knelt by the bed and began to pray in Spanish. He included the officer's family in his prayer. The offi-

Latin America: Where EE Really Exploded

cer was so moved, he took off his gun and belt and knelt next to Woody. As Woody continued in prayer, he put his arm around the officer.

When he was through praying, Woody asked the officer EE's two diagnostic questions and proceeded to lead the man to Christ!

The officer requested the list of pastors Woody was to see and their phone numbers. While Woody was showering, the officer telephoned each of the pastors, *ordering* them to come to Woody's room at the hotel. Of course, the pastors didn't dare not show up! Woody met with them, one-by-one, telling them about EE. Many of those pastors, still active in the ministry today, yet remember Woody's first visit to their country. That's how EE got its start in Nicaragua!

When Woody Lajara first visited Havana to share in an EE clinic, a bomb exploded in the hotel where he was staying. Immediately, the authorities closed all the building's entrances. Suddenly Woody found his room full of military people. One of the officers held in his hand the EE training manual.

"What is this manual for? Making *explosives?*"

Woody was quick to seize the opportunity. "Let me explain!" he offered, and shared with them the Gospel. Two of the officers, on the spot, accepted Christ as their Savior, and Woody was granted freedom to continue his ministry!

Good Local Leadership

In addition to such zeal to witness, the Holy Spirit has given Woody Lajara an unusual gift for presenting the EE ministry to key evangelical leaders throughout Latin America. He has many key contacts all over the continent who, like him, were youth leaders in the 1980s. Some of them grew up with Woody;

they participated with him in continental Christian gatherings and have been his friends for many years.

These men and women had been searching for a course that would train the rank-and-file laity in their churches to witness effectively. Many times, as Woody visited a local church and assured the pastor that EE "works," the pastor responded with a "Show me!" So Woody would take the pastor out onto the streets and parks and let them watch him share the Gospel and lead someone to Christ. It was very evident from these demonstrations that EE indeed "worked," and when Woody invited pastors and key leaders to attend a clinic (at which he was the teacher/trainer), they accepted eagerly.

Mission boards and denominational leaders, likewise, gave strong recognition to the ministry. They saw that EE was a ministry based on biblical principles, very deeply rooted in the Word of God. It was and is a ministry to help the leadership of local churches train the laity in their churches. Those leaders could see clearly that it was a local-church-based ministry and not a competing para-church organization.

There is still another factor that accounts, under God, for EE's great success in Latin America. *It brings results!* Local churches implementing EE began to grow. Some of them experienced remarkable growth. One church grew from 80 members to 800 in the space of two years. An Assemblies of God church in Caracas grew from 30 to 80, then to 200, then to 600, in two years. They had to purchase the properties around them to enlarge their sanctuary. A church in Barranquilla, Colombia, grew from 7 members to 5,000 in just five years. The pastor of Centro Internacional de Alabanza Church reported his church added 1,345 new Christians just through on-the-job training visits. The church added 1,280 more as EE-trained people practiced EE as "a way of life."

Latin America: Where EE Really Exploded

In Puerto Rico, the Balboa Presbyterian Church conducts a clinic every year. This is one of the fastest growing Presbyterian churches in Puerto Rico. According to the Synod, "the churches experiencing healthy growth are those implementing EE." In Buenos Aires, Argentina, I met one pastor who told me that, largely through EE, he has seen his church grow from 750 members in 1984 to 12,000 today!

EE Beginnings

The ministry of EE in Latin America officially started with the translation of the training material into Spanish in 1980. Estri Britton, a missionary pastor from one of the Lesser Antilles, had begun the translation from English into Spanish. But as his obligations increased, he had to stop. In 1980, when Woody became Vice President for Latin American, his first task was to finish the translation Estri had started.

Woody and his associates put together a very good translation. After four years of working together like that, some of them elected to become part of a newly developing "EE Latin American Team."

God provided funds for scholarships so that many key evangelical leaders in Latin America could attend clinics in the United States. Those leaders were committed to go back and help Woody organize the ministry in their countries.

About that time the continental vice presidents, led by Archie Parrish, designed a process to introduce EE into a new country. This was approved by the Board and was extremely helpful! First, God helped EE in each country organize a "Contact Group." This eventually evolved into what was called a "National Advisory Council." Later, with further ministry maturity, it became a "National Board of Directors." Following those steps down to the "last jot and tittle," Woody began introducing EE into country after country throughout Latin America. In some countries the ministry did not grow very much until years later. But by the year 1983, EE had been planted in every Latin American country.

In 1982, the first clinic was held in Puerto Rico at the First Baptist Church of Carolina with 65 people attending. "Since this was the first clinic," Woody explained, "we selected the participants, 50 percent pastors and 50 percent laymen." Woody was the senior clinic teacher, assisted by Rev. Jose Castro, the local pastor in charge of evangelism, and a lay teacher trainer from Monterey, Mexico.

The same year, clinics were held in Monterey (Mexico), Bogota (Colombia), and Caracas (Venezuela). The number of participants in those clinics varied from 65 to 85. The excitement of the participants was remarkable, and 85 percent of them went back to their local churches and implemented the ministry with amazing results! Every church that implemented EE multiplied literally by the hundreds. For example, the Church in Carolina, Puerto Rico, grew from 1,700 to 4,000 and the Las Acasias Church in Caracas, Venezuela, in a matter of two or three years, from 300 to 1,300!

The initial response to EE from pastors as well as from local churches was very positive. Entire denominations selected EE as their official tool to train their constituency in evangelism. In fact, the demand became so great that the number of registrations had to be limited. Some clinics had to close registrations two or three months before the opening date.

During the time Woody served as International Executive Vice President, two other Continental Vice Presidents served briefly: Dr. Wilfred Estrada and Rev. James E. Brumet.

Throughout Latin America, from three clinics held in 1982,

Latin America: The Explosion Has Been Dramatic

the number has grown to over 100 each year for the last three years. Since the beginning, a total of 934 clinics have been held, equipping approximately 37,360 pastors and lay persons. At last count, 3,450 churches throughout the continent have been equipped with EE. Of those churches actually involved in EE, 1,260 churches are still implementing EE at this time. Many churches don't keep records, and guerrilla activity in nations such as Colombia has been disruptive, but it can be safely estimated that at least 175,000 persons in Latin America have been EE-equipped and some 1.5 million to 3 million people have come to Jesus Christ through local church EE ministries.

From the beginning to 1989, excitement was high and growth remained steady. Hundreds of churches started EE with good success. In order to satisfy the demand, materials had to be published in seven different countries. Many denominations and local independent churches used EE as the "perfect tool to plant new churches." One church in Argentina planted 22 new congregations.

Following the approved process for introducing EE into new nations, Woody established the first National Advisory Boards: an eight-member Board in Venezuela and a five-member board in Colombia. Within a year or two, National Boards of Advisors had been established in practically every country of the continent.

The Christian and Missionary Alliance loaned missionary Rev. Robert Searing to serve as part-time director of EE Colombia. Since he was born of missionary parents serving there, Bob had been a missionary in Colombia all of his life. Bishop Joel Mora was appointed as Director for Mexico; Osvaldo C. Casati as director for Argentina. John Abel, a Lutheran missionary, was appointed Director for Brazil. This group of leaders became the first EE "Latin American Team."

Other key leaders need to be mentioned: Samuel Olson in Venezuela; Rich Davis in Peru; Eddie Jakob and Pepe Mardones in Chile; Juan Calcagni in Argentina; Joaquim de Paula Rosa, Joelcio Barreto and Rivas Brettones in Brazil; Nahum Vega, David Arevalo and Santiago Marin, in Mexico.

Due to the many minority groups throughout Latin America, Woody's "Latin America Team" asked the Lord to bring one qualified person to oversee this area. Instead, God brought two! He brought Rev. David Gomez, a Guatemalan pastor, and Eleanore Beach, a Wycliffe missionary. Eleanore and her husband, Ed, were involved in the translation of the Bible into one of the ethnic languages of Guatemala. Eleanore became very excited about EE and trained David in their local church. They saw so much fruit, they decided to translate EE into the Tectiteco language. So the Ethnic Ministry began with their vision and interest.

In four years, David, Eleanore and Ed have been able to translate the basic EE material and some of the booklets into seven languages. They have also provided EE training to pastors and lay people in those ethnic groups. Now, they are working to translate EE materials into another 15 languages. They have produced a key manual to teach Christians how to work with ethnic groups.

Outreach

EE Churches in Latin America have also reached out to other nations. For example, in 1995, First Baptist Church in Satelite, Mexico, was inspired to provide six scholarships for Cuban pastors to attend their clinic. When those Cuban pastors returned home, some of them started EE in their local churches. One pastor, Rev. Felipe Rodriguez, had remarkable success in his church in Havana. Two years later the first EE clinic in Cuba took place in his church. To date, over 20 clinics have been held in Cuba.

Over 300 national pastors and lay leaders have been trained and are actively putting EE to work. It is estimated that over 20,000 Cubans have come to know Jesus as their personal Savior, thanks to the vision of that one church in Mexico City!

Other key leaders have motivated their local churches to help start EE in another country. A church in Puerto Rico helped introduce EE in the Dominican Republic.

Colombian churches helped greatly in the development of EE in Ecuador and Bolivia, and churches in Brazil have helped launch EE in Portugal.

There isn't adequate space to cover every nation in Latin America. We will look, therefore, at just a few nations and areas representative of what God is doing throughout Latin America.

Colombia

Evangelism Explosion was launched in Colombia in 1983 by Rev. Robert (Bob) M. Searing, Jr. Upon returning from furlough, Bob secured some Spanish copies of the EE textbook and workbooks and began training new Christians in the Encounter Church he and his wife Marge had just started in Bogota.

At the same time, Bob encouraged four pastors and leaders to go to an English-Spanish clinic being offered in Miami. The four men attended that clinic and returned to Bogota to start EE in their churches.

By the middle of 1984 the Encounter Church had a group of about 25 people trained. The first clinic was held at that church in February 1985, with 71 pastors and leaders attending.

That same year, a five-member Colombia Board of Directors was established, with Bob appointed as Colombia's first director. Since that first clinic, EE Colombia has held 131 clinics in the cities of Bogota, Ibague, Cali, Cuscue, Puerto Asis, Barranguilla. Colombian pastors had been looking for a course that would teach their people to evangelize; so EE was well received. Several churches in Bogota, Ibague and Cali became very committed to EE and spread the news to other churches.

Clinics continued to grow, but EE in the individual churches waned. Two factors, in large part, brought about this shift. First, guerrilla warfare seriously affected Colombia's economy and EE's ability to help the churches financially. Second, a new "instant growth" mentality in the evangelical churches steered them away from methods of evangelism such as EE that require time to disciple new believers.

All told, some 140 Colombian churches have implemented EE, training more than 21,000 people. Many churches do not or cannot report the people won to Christ through EE, but estimates put the figure between 250,000 and 500,000.

EE Colombia helped neighboring countries launch and implement the ministry. For several years they helped Ecuador by providing materials and teachers for their clinics. They shipped materials to a church in Bolivia. They provided materials for Costa Rica and helped teach in their first clinics. They brought pastors from Costa Rica, Honduras, and Guatemala for training in Colombian churches and clinics. They provided materials for Cuba, Dominican Republic, Peru, and Chile to start EE ministries in those countries.

Growth in Colombian churches through EE is proof that EE works in the Latin American context. Centro de Alabanza church in Barranquilla grew from seven members to more than 5,000 in five years through the use of EE.

Latin America: The Explosion Has Been Dramatic

When it comes to Kids' EE, Colombia is leading the charge in Latin America. On a five-day visit to Bogota I met some very unusual children at the Filadelfia Church. Age 8 to 12, they were all trained in Kids' EE. On that occasion, they were singing in a Kids' EE chorus to celebrate the 16th anniversary of the ministry's entry into Colombia.

One child who caught my attention was 12-year-old Monica. Two years earlier, after taking an experimental children's EE course, Monica personally led 80 people to Christ, young and old, during two-hour bus trips from her home in the country to school in the city. The EE pastor from her church began a daughter church with those new believers. Today, over 130 attend that church, all because a ten-year-old, trained in EE, shared her faith!

Brazil

In 1980, Woody Lajara made a trip to Sao Paulo, Brazil. His purpose was to establish a National Advisory Council that would take ownership for the development of EE in Brazil. What he found was interest in the EE ministry generated by the 1975 publishing of a Portuguese version of Dr. Kennedy's book, *Evangelism Explosion*. He also found a few missionaries who had been EE-trained in the United Sates.

Woody invited three of the pastors, who spoke English, to a clinic in the United States. After training, they would formally launch EE in their churches and prepare for the first Portuguese-language clinic. Woody asked another member of the core group, John Abel, a Free Lutheran missionary, to translate the training material and help prepare for the clinic.

In October 1983 the first EE clinic was held in Sao Paulo, hosted by Pastor Rivas L. Bretones and his Brooklyn Baptist

Church. The next Spring another clinic followed at the Second Baptist Church of Campos, Rio de Janeiro. Meanwhile, back in the United States the Lord was calling a full-time missionary to coordinate the ministry of EE Brazil. Robert Foster and his wife, Mary Jo, both of them lay EE trainers who had made two short-term trips to Brazil, heard a call to missions. By October 1985 they had raised their personal support and relocated in Sao Paulo, where they began a year of language study. In 1987 Robert became full-time Regional Coordinator, with a national office in Sao Paulo.

Since 1997, Rev. Jose, Carlos Ribeiro, a Brazilian, has been full-time Regional Director for EE-Brazil, which has grown significantly under his leadership. During 2001 alone, the ministry held 17 clinics across Brazil. Since 1983, 130 clinics have been held in Brazil with some 2,000 pastors and 3,500 lay people certified.

Caribbean

In March 1988, Rev. Jack Hawthorne was appointed as EE Director of Caribbean Ministries. His wife, Fairy, served as his Administrative Assistant. First, they had to raise funds for support, scholarships, printing, ministry and travel. Then they worked to get acquainted with leaders in the Caribbean nations. The latter was done by island-hopping trips, beginning with an 18-country trip in March 1989. At least one such extended trip was taken each year and many shorter ones as needed.

On those trips Jack would make a phone call to a recommended pastor on an island, asking him to make arrangements for meeting other pastors. This usually worked very well, but his first visit to St. Maarten was memorable. He had called in advance and made arrangements with a Rev. Romney to meet

Latin America: The Explosion Has Been Dramatic

his plane, arrange housing and call a meeting of local pastors. He arrived in St. Maarten on schedule, but no one was there to meet him. Jack called Rev. Romney, but the man answering said he was not Pastor Romney. He "wasn't even 'religious!'"

He apparently thought it was amusing to have led Jack on when he called a wrong number from the States. Obviously, the "real" Pastor Romney did not know anything about Jack's coming, had contacted no pastors and had arranged no place for Jack to stay.

So Jack hailed a cab, led the cab driver to the Lord, found a hotel room, walked the streets for hours, made lots of phone calls, and when he left St. Maartens he felt that much had been accomplished. (Incidentally, the "real" Pastor Romney became an EE supporter. Before too long, EE was being taught in St. Maartin in three languages.)

When the Hawthornes began, there were four pastors in Barbados and one in Nassau who had been trained in U.S. clinics. EE was going well in San Andres, where the first Caribbean clinic was held in 1988. At first, Caribbean leaders were brought to U.S. clinics. Then, as pastors returned home to start EE in their churches, "missionary clinics" with volunteer clinic teachers and trainers from the U.S. were held in EE-interested churches. In 1989 four of these clinics were scheduled in Nassau, Kingston/Mandeville, Jamaica and St. Croix, but Hurricane Hugo postponed the St. Croix clinic. Six clinics were held in 1990, and the number grew to 15 in 1993.

In 1991 Jack invited me to bring a short-term missions team to Barbados and teach an EE clinic at the Abundant Life Assembly. I had an opportunity to observe first-hand the impact of EE upon one of the most dynamic and growing churches in the Caribbean. Since then, the EE ministry and Abundant Life Assembly have continued to grow. The number

Explosion of Evangelism

of church's certified EE trainers is now above 300! By 1995, 14 clinics were held in the Caribbean, including the first one in Haiti. Most of the clinics were taught by certified Caribbean clinic teachers. Clinics were conducted in English, Spanish, French, Dutch and Papiamentu. A three-weekend clinic schedule was developed to meet the need for training bi-vocational Caribbean pastors.

In 1992, EE ministries began in Dominica, Grenada, Montserrat, Turks and Caicos. That completed the list of 26 non-Hispanic Caribbean nations and territories implementing the ministry.

The positive response to the Gospel presentation in all Caribbean countries has been high—between 62 percent in French countries (surprisingly higher than leaders expected) and 80-90 percent in most other countries. In the spring of 1991, a French translation of all the EE materials was completed and printed. In the fall of 1992 the materials were produced in Papiamentu, the Dutch Creole spoken in Suriname. In February 1994, the Dutch translation of the training materials was finished. In the summer of 1995, leaders in Suriname also completed translating the EE textbook into Dutch.

In June 1994, the first All-Caribbean Leadership Conference was held at a commodious university campus in Barbados. Dr. Kennedy came as one of the key speakers. A number of Caribbean leaders led workshops and planning sessions; national leaders became acquainted and made plans for future ministry.

In late 1995 Jack and Fairy Hawthorne, after very fruitful years of pioneer Caribbean ministry, retired. Tim McGlame succeeded the Hawthornes. Under Tim's administration, the Caribbean EE ministry continued to grow. Today a Puerto Rican, Will Rodriguez, is the Caribbean Director. Will found Christ through EE and has come up through the ranks. Speaking fluent English and Spanish, Will has proven to be an excellent choice to minister on islands where both languages are used. The ministry continues to grow and bear abundant fruit.

You thought we had covered the continents (except for Antarctica), and in a sense we have. But there remains another exciting world area that falls across both Europe and Asia—the former Soviet Union, now known as the Commonwealth of Independent States (C.I.S.). For convenience, EE calls it Eurasia. EE is very much there, playing its customary role in bringing people to Christ Jesus, the Savior. EE Eurasia is a fascinating and exciting part of the EE story. We tell you about it in the chapter that follows.

Eurasia
Rev. Buddy Gaines
Vice President, Eurasia

*"Our youth were in spiritual crisis;
then EE gave them zeal for evangelism."*
- Eldar and Merab, Georgia, C.I.S.

"This EE ministry has brought life into our youth group."
- Pastor Anataliji Muhin, Russia

Chapter 10

Eurasia: A New Day of Opportunity

THE DATE WAS May 3, 1993. Rev. Buddy Gaines, the indomitable man we met before in this survey of Evangelism Explosion, was about to make more history. In Ukraine for an EE clinic, Buddy had a meeting that morning at 10 o'clock with a Dr. Nickolay Revtov. Dr. Revtov was the leading professor of metallurgy at Priazzovsky Technical University, Mariupol, Ukraine. He was also the school's vice rector in line to be the university's president.

At the appointed hour, Buddy and his Russian interpreter, Natasha Kulishova, a friend of Dr. Revtov, were ushered into the doctor's large office. Their mission: to present the Gospel to this disenchanted Communist.

Nickolay Revtov had been a card-carrying Communist for 23 years. He had four earned doctorates. Buddy was surprised how youthful he looked. The collapse of Communism two years earlier had left Nickolay Revtov disillusioned. Then he and his wife, Olga, read in the local newspaper that free Russian-language Bibles were available from an organization in Vienna,

Austria. They sent for one and began reading it. In their entire lives, neither had ever gone to church. Although they did not fully understand the Bible they were reading, they hungered for spiritual truth.

Natasha Kulishova, the interpreter and friend of Nickolay, introduced Buddy, informing him of Nickolay's interest in Christianity.

"For two hours that morning," Buddy says, "I shared the Good News of Jesus Christ with this searching man. Several times the telephone interrupted. Finally, Dr. Revtov disconnected it. His secretary came in several times until he closed and locked the door!

"It was nearing noon when I completed the presentation of the Gospel. 'Does this make sense to you, Dr. Revtov?' I asked.

"'Yes, it does!' he responded.

"'Would you like to receive the free gift of eternal life now?' I continued.

"'Yes, I would!' So we prayed and he trusted Christ and Christ alone for his personal salvation and for the free gift of eternal life!

"I shared with Nickolay Revtov a few immediate follow-up items, and then it was time for me to hurry to my teaching assignment at the first EE clinic in newly-freed Ukraine. Before we left his office, however, Dr. Revtov invited me to visit him at his home that Friday evening. He wanted me to share what I had told him with his wife, Olga, and his 15-year-old son, Sasha!

"I taught in the clinic that entire week, all the time anticipating the Friday night visit at the home of Nickolay Revtov. Friday evening came, and I took with me an interpreter and two other EE teammates. Dr. Revtov was in front of his house awaiting our arrival. He ushered us inside. After removing our shoes we entered the parlor, where coffee, tea, and cakes were arranged on the coffee table.

"Olga, Nickolay's wife, had invited a friend to hear the Gospel, too. And the Revtov's 15-year-old son, Sasha, was also there. After socializing for a while I began to work through the conversational introduction of the EE presentation.

"Olga's friend interrupted, 'We were comfortable as communists, but it's failed. Can your President help us?' I said, 'I don't represent the President. I speak for Jesus Christ who offers you the gift of eternal life.'

"With that, I gave an explanation of the Gospel, and that night, all three of them—Olga, Sasha and Olga's friend—prayed to receive the free gift of eternal life. It would be hard to say who was happiest: the new believers, the Ukrainian evangelists I was training, or I, the American, seeing yet again the amazing way God was opening doors of opportunity in the former Soviet Union.

"'Three months later I returned to Mariupol, Ukraine, to teach the second semester of the clinic. I was told that Nickolay, Ogla, and Sasha, the very next Sunday, had begun attending Central Baptist Church. All three were preparing to be baptized in September 1993."

Unmistakable Calling

"I learned something else when I revisited Mariupol to teach the second semester of the clinic. Nickolay Revtov believed God was leading him into full-time Christian ministry! In fact, Nickolay's pastor was sending him to our EE clinic. He wanted me to disciple and advise Nickolay. Imagine! A man with four earned doctorates wanting to study the Bible and theology.

"With a new-found passion for sharing his faith, Nickolay Revtov quickly mastered the EE material. During the clinic, Nickolay was on my team all three nights of on-the-job training. As we went out the third night, Nickolay shared the Gospel and led two people to Christ. At the time, he himself was a three-months-old "baby"!

"In October I requested that he join me in Moscow to meet a man interested in helping us spread EE across the former Soviet Union. We worked together introducing EE to pastors in Moscow.

"Then he and I flew to the city of Omsk in Siberia to conduct an EE clinic. As a young Christian man, Nickolay served as my associate teacher. He taught with eloquence and style, and he was well received.

"In February 1994, Nickolay traveled to China to teach metallurgy to students at Shen-yang University. He shared the Gospel with many who had never heard the Good News. He returned home in July to teach another clinic. It was hard to believe the energy level of this new Christian who had done so much in so short a time!

"During that week of teaching together, Nickolay asked if he might speak to me privately. I wondered what might be coming. Of course, I was glad to make time for him.

"'I believe God is calling me into pastoral ministry,' Nicholay confided. He was then a candidate for the presidency of his university, a high honor. But he was already sensing a greater allegiance to his new-found Lord."

Eurasian Director

Nickolay Revtov began serving as Director for EE Eurasia in September 1994. Before that, in August 1994, he resigned his post at the university in Mariupol, Ukraine. I recalled the message he had faxed to me some time before: 'Buddy, I have given my life to metals and Communism. Now I want to serve only Jesus Christ through Evangelism Explosion!'"

Karl Marx once wrote, "My main purpose is to destroy all the world and to be equal to God." With the demise of the Soviet Union more than a decade ago, Marx's failure became universally evident. But the fervor of his beliefs shaped generations of Russians. Today, some former Communists are now using that same intensity of purpose to share Christ with a troubled nation. Nickolay Revtov is one of them.

There's much to accomplish in a vast land that spans 11 time zones and includes nearly 300 million people. Some of the former USSR's republics are virtually unreached. For example, Turkmenistan, a Muslim nation of four million people, has only two churches. They share one pastor. In Tajikstan there is no pastor and only one deacon to shepherd the only two churches that currently exist.

Evangelism Explosion, known in the Commonwealth of Independent States as "Heart-to-Heart EE," is working effectively to both evangelize and disciple people in places where the evangelical church is small or non-existent.

Three years after the iron curtain opened, Buddy Gaines, by then EE's International Vice President, wrote, "Although my office is at EE headquarters in Fort Lauderdale, one-third of my time is spent in the former Soviet Union . . . . The ministry opportunities for EE training continue to grow in these former communist countries. To help us concentrate more closely on this needy area, we have formed a 'seventh continent' which we are calling Eurasia."

That "seventh continent" includes the following twelve nations: Moldova, Russia, Ukraine, Uzbekistan, Armenia,

Azerbaijan, Belarus, Georgia, Kazakhstan, Kyrgyzstan, Tajikistan and Turkmenistan.

Amazing Beginnings

The ministry of EE was first introduced to the Russian world in August 1992, in the city of Irkutsk, Siberia. The indefatigable Buddy Gaines and his wife, Martie, went together to conduct the first EE seminar/clinic in Russia. About 50 people, mostly pastors and lay leaders, took the course. To them, it was an absolutely new method of sharing the Gospel. Because it was an "American import," it was somewhat controversial.

In March 1993, Buddy conducted an EE clinic in Moscow, and in May the first EE clinic in Ukraine at Mariupol (mentioned earlier in this chapter). Buddy Gaines's efforts to plant EE in all parts of the C.I.S. are matched, and possibly exceeded, by the great ability God has given him to raise up leaders for EE! Nickolay Revtov is one of many quality people Buddy has discipled and mentored for Christian service. Nickolay Revtov is a picture of what God is doing in that entire region. This is an incredible time in the spiritual history of that part of the world. EE is thrilled to be a part of it!

In the midst of a very exciting ministry and exhaustive travel, Nickolay Revtov paused long enough to put in writing some of his thoughts. Here is what he wrote:

"We know from the Bible that godly people changed the lives of millions, because they allowed God to use them for His purpose. God always reaches His goal. The question is, whom will He use? I remember when I was a young Communist I wanted to change the world.

"I wanted to build Communism on earth. Fortunately, I

couldn't do it. I tried to change my country, but I couldn't do it. Then I tried to change my city, my university and my family. But I failed. I could change nothing.

"When I placed my trust in Jesus Christ and became a Christian, God used me to change my family, my university, the lives of many people in my city and my country. Now He is using me to change the lives of many people through Heart-to-Heart EE in Eurasia, and I praise and thank Him for this responsibility and privilege."

An Update on the Family

EE, in turn, praises God for Nickolay, his wife Olga, and their two sons, Andrew and Sasha. The younger, Sasha, is now studying for the ministry at Criswell Bible College in Dallas, Texas. Two years after his parents' conversion, Andrew, their older son, returned home, his marriage broken, and hounded by other problems. He was converted May 7, 1995, exactly two years from the night his mother and brother trusted Christ! Andrew has studied in a Bible college and is now an ordained pastor in Ukraine and serves as director for Youth EE in Eurasia. He plans to earn a doctorate in theology.

Nickolay Revtov, now a graduate in theological studies and an ordained pastor, serves as full-time Director of EE Eurasia. Recently he wrote:

"Just recently I had an opportunity with God's help to go across all of the former USSR. I traveled from Khabarovsk, in the Far East, to Brest, the point farthest west of the former Soviet Union. This kind of traveling allowed me to see how much people need our Lord Jesus Christ. From Brest to Kamchatka Peninsula, from Dikson (farthest north) to Kushka (farthest south) everywhere people need the Gospel of Jesus Christ.

"God has blessed Heart-to-Heart EE. Literally thousands of people have turned to God. Our five EE centers in Eurasia effectively help the development of this ministry in different C.I.S. regions. We thank God for EE coordinators, teachers and trainers. We thank God for the thousands of faithful, Spirit-led brothers and sisters who, from heart to heart, are bringing the Good News to people in all of the C.I.S."

Nickolay and Olga are in the process of moving from Mariupol to Kiev, the capital of Ukraine. They asked God to help them sell their house, and it sold. God provided a beautiful property in Irpen, a suburb of Kiev. Even more recently, God has provided to EE Eurasia a substantial three-story building just a three-minute walk from the current office location in Irpen. The new facility will accommodate Heart-to-Heart EE's international expansion and make possible several new ministry divisions, including Kids' EE, Youth EE, Adult EE, Seniors' EE and Prison EE.

Kids' EE

Speaking of Kids' EE, this is something very new to Eurasia. Alexander Knyazkov, in Kazakhstan, reports, "During spring holidays, our church organized a vacation Bible school whose main purpose was to teach 'the smallest of us' the Heart-to-Heart EE method of evangelism.

"We needed materials, but they were not translated. The easiest language for the kids is the language of comics. Our brothers adapted materials into this language, and all we had to do was copy them.

"All the children received the materials! If anybody came into Galbory Church during those three days, he could hear the bouncing of a basketball. The director of the Bible school, Chernyak Tatyana Petrovna, was throwing the ball to a child asking 'Heaven is _____?' The child catching the ball had to answer, 'A free gift!' The child was also supposed to recite a verse from the Bible to help him or her remember the Gospel outline.

"Thirty children, from six to twelve, and five teachers participated. Teaching was done with the help of skits the children themselves performed. Four of the children prayed to receive the gift of eternal life! Now the army of Christians here will be reinforced with its youngest soldier-witnesses!"

In January 2002, Kids' EE was officially introduced to Heart-to-Heart EE coordinators. A total of ten Kids' EE clinics are planned for the year 2002.

Youth EE

On April 14-19, 2000, for the first time in Russia, a clinic for youth leaders was conducted in Siberia. Andrew Revtov, EE Clinic Teacher, reported that there were 47 people from five regions of Siberia, representing 28 churches and 15 cities. At first, Andrew said those enrolled in the clinic were apprehensive because of all the detail and memorization.

"But after the first on-the-job training," Andrew added, "everything was cleared up. Many participants remarked, 'It was exactly what our ministry needed. It was what we were looking for!' They thanked God for the opportunity to be there. During three days of on-the-job visits, 122 people heard the Gospel and 40 of them prayed the sinner's prayer."

Andrew went on to say that the youth leaders saw how God could use them for His glory and the service of His church. Better yet, the clinic was an answer to the "purpose" question. Many leaders had been asking, "Now that we have the youth coming to church, what do we do with them?" The answer: Turn them loose to win friends and classmates to Christ! Get them excited about evangelism!

One Siberian pastor commented, "Youth are not the *future* of the church. They are its *present*." Rick Bond, Vice President for Youth EE, introduced Youth EE to Ukraine. Now national leaders throughout Eurasia are doing Youth EE.

Translation

Early in the ministry of Heart-to-Heart EE in Russia, a group of missionaries and Russians attempted to translate the EE materials into Russian. But it was a poor translation. Providentially, God raised up a gifted woman, Natasha Kulishova, who taught English in the University of Mariupol, Ukraine. After attending an EE clinic in Birmingham, Alabama, she revised the earlier, poor translation.

Later, Nickolay Revtov added further refinements to the printed material. Subsequently, the basic EE materials have been translated and published in Ukrainian, Armenian, Georgian, Azerii, Uzbekian, Turkmenian, Kazakhian, Kyrgyian and Yakutian.

In Azerbaijan, the Heart-to-Heart EE coordinator, Alekper Kasimov, rejoiced when the translated materials were in his Azerii tongue. "Now," he exclaimed, "by God's blessing, we can teach EE in our national language in all the churches of our nation!"

Leadership

The first Advisory Council in Ukraine was established in 1993 with four members. As the ministry grew, so did the council. In fact, Ukraine Heart-to-Heart EE has become a model for the other C.I.S. nations. But that doesn't mean Ukraine EE is resting on its laurels. The Council is still concerned about "raising the quality of the teaching and assisting further development of the 16-week training courses."

Nickolay Revtov finds it "encouraging" to watch EE grow and mature in the other C.I.S. nations. By now there are advisory councils in most of them. And, as the ministry has grown, God has added leaders. The EE Eurasia staff includes 21 coordinators covering Central Asia, the Caucasus region, Ukraine, Moldova, European Russia, Belarus and all of Siberian Russia.

At first, some pastors thought EE was too much an America import and not applicable to Russia. But many openly welcomed the training, exclaiming, "This is exactly what our churches need!" Now 349 churches across Eurasia use EE to equip their members. Some are even using it to plant new churches. At least 60 such churches have been started.

More and more pastors and churches are coming to realize that in Eurasia there are two effective ways to develop evangelism. One is to train laymen for personal heart-to-heart evangelism. The other is to combine all other types of evangelism with personal heart-to-heart evangelism. This means that EE should be an integral part of whatever type of evangelism a church or a nation elects to employ.

Konstantine Galaiko, Coordinator for Ukraine Heart-to-Heart EE, compares EE with the mass evangelism campaigns that followed the Soviet disintegration. "The years of collapse and rebuilding allowed the churches of Irkutsk to hold huge Gospel meetings in the palaces and stadiums. Thousands of our citizens heard the Gospel's saving news, but only a very few of these people later came to a church. The beautiful chorus songs, the poems and the sermons do not guarantee that the soul of a person will turn to God. Personal conversation between believers and unbelievers is essential. Heart-to-Heart EE ministry gives us this."

Encouraging Statistics

In the past ten years, EE Eurasia has seen amazing growth in the number of EE Leadership Training clinics—from 2 clinics to 93 this past year. And how effective have these clinics been? Here is the testimony of Pastor Dmitry Bahteev from Kpstroma, Russia:

"Many godly people said that 1999 would be the year of spiritual revival in Russia. I was praying about my city and asked God to show me His plans and use me to fulfill them. One evening, I received a phone call from a fellow pastor, inviting me to attend an EE clinic.

"So I went along with two members of my congregation. During the course of the clinic I saw Christ's Great Commission from a different point of view. God showed the three of us a way to bring the Gospel to our city.

"Back home again, I organized three teams. For two months we trained these teams to share the Gospel. Then we walked around the city and 'fished.' Little by little fear and uncertainty were replaced by freedom to proclaim the Good News. And God has blessed this ministry. Within several weeks, we had presented the Gospel to 71 people, and 49 of them received Jesus Christ as Lord of their lives."

Since the start of Heart-to-Heart EE in Eurasia, some 13,000 pastors and lay leaders have been trained in EE. And an estimated 30,000 persons have come to Christ through the ministry. Dozens of seminars and conferences have been held.

Eurasia: A New Day of Opportunity

The first Clinic Teachers Conference took place in June, 1997. In July 2002, EE Eurasia will celebrate its ten-year anniversary.

Difficult Circumstances

The launching and spreading of EE in Eurasia has not been easy. Just the distribution of EE materials can be a challenge. Eurasia does not have an efficient postal system. Often the materials must be sent by rail. Even then, the only secure way is to ask passengers to personally deliver the materials. In some Muslim areas, such as Azerbaijan, materials must be sent secretly.

Travel is also difficult. Clinic teacher Alexander Bondar describes a trip to teach a clinic in Bishkek, Kazakhstan: "Police stopped us on our way to the Kazakhstan border. They took us to the police headquarters to examine us. When they discovered we had a computer, we had to wait for the computer specialist to arrive and check the computer. They said many groups were using computers to print anti-government brochures. We were held up for five hours before they let us proceed."

At a clinic in Central Asia, organizers wondered if participants would arrive. Several days prior to the meeting, an extreme Islamic group had come down from the mountains. The group shot several hunters and then several policemen in a border town that clinic participants would pass through. God answered prayer. All of the conference participants arrived safely.

EE Coordinator Igor Markov relates difficulties encountered in Bryansk, Russia: "The very first day of on-the-job training, the teams went to do questionnaires. On one team was a trainee who needed to make an urgent telephone call to his home, so the trainer led his group the post office (post offices in Russia generally have public telephones). While the one clinician telephoned, the others were evangelizing.

"Their evangelizing drew the attention of the police. They had no identification with them, so the police took the group to the nearest militia office. By law they could have been detained two days. The trainer began to explain who they were, what they were doing, and where they lived. The militia officer did not want to let them go, but when they began to present the Gospel, his attitude changed. The team did not make a convert of the militia officer, but he did let the group go!"

Difficult Places

Possibly the two hardest places to do EE are in Siberia and the Arctic. EE Eurasia is bearing fruit in both of them!

Alexander Gollandtsev testifies: "I participated in an EE clinic in Irkutsk, Central Siberia. During the clinic I saw people receiving Jesus. In EE, God has given His church a strong spiritual weapon. This ministry lives up to its name. It is explosive!

"On the way home by train, a Christian brother and I shared the Gospel with an elderly woman in the train corridor. She repented and invited Christ into her heart. Afterward, she said, 'It is so sad that nobody in my village told me about God as simply as you did.'

"After my return home, God helped me to develop the Heart-to-Heart EE ministry in my church. Within two months we were doing on-the-job training. Five people repented. I have not seen a better evangelistic method than Heart-to-Heart EE."

Probably the very most difficult place to take EE is above the Arctic Circle. Winter temperatures 50 degrees below zero are not uncommon. There are two modes of transportation. In the summer, helicopters. In the winter, cars, using the frozen rivers as roads. It took three years to implement EE in the huge territory of Yakutia, equal in size to France, Germany and Italy combined.

EE Works!

In Eurasia, too, the testimonies of many bear witness to the practicality of EE. Pastor Korotash Peter likes the ease of the presentation and the clinic's "family-like atmosphere." He says, "Every day we go from theory to practice. The greatest encouragement is to see a person make a decision to turn to God."

Deacon Konstantine Shova remarks, "I have learned a clear and structured presentation of the Gospel. This brings discipline to the speaker. It allows the hearer to weigh the issues before making a decision."

Peter Dotsin, another pastor, states, "I have shared the Good News many times, but discovered that I was making a big mistake. Conversations turned out to be monologues, not dialogues. I pushed people away. I would guess that many preachers are in need of this method of evangelism. The future belongs to EE. It is especially effective."

Irina Tiraspol, a Youth Worker, says she is at a loss for words. "EE is truly an 'explosion,' a thunder in the clear sky. I had no idea that I could so easily and simply talk to people about the Good News. I came to the clinic with a desire to learn how to share Christ with people. I didn't expect the training would let me rethink the Gospel and understand the heart of the Great Commission."

There you have it. Forty years. Every continent (except Antarctica). Every nation. Every territory. *But not yet every person.*

Read on to learn why we at Evangelism Explosion are convinced we must not stop midway in the task of world evangelization. By his life and leadership, Dr. D. James Kennedy has pointed the way. In Evangelism Explosion, Dr. Kennedy has given the world a practical method of personal evangelism.

Evangelism Explosion involves prayer, purpose, certain principles and, of course, people. The concluding chapter speaks about these priorities and ends with a legacy of guidelines Dr. Kennedy articulates for the future.

March 1996 – EE celebrates being the first Christian ministry in every nation.

"EE is the most effective tool we have for
reaching the youth of this nation."
- EE pastor, Indonesia

"It's awesome to be equipped to share the gospel, not only on EE
nights, but whenever the opportunity is there!"
- Mark Neumann, USA

Chapter 11

The Decade Ahead

IN 1996 DELEGATES from all over the world gathered in Fort Lauderdale to celebrate EE's entry into every nation. And in the year 2000 we rejoiced that EE was in every territory. But one thing needs to be made clear: We do not view these achievements as a conclusion.

Rather, we see them as a beginning, a beachhead, a launching pad for a far wider, deeper, stronger thrust into every one of those nations and territories. Truly fulfilling the Great Commission requires that every corner of the globe and every people group be reached with the Gospel—an enormous task that dwarfs that of "reaching" all the nations.

Jesus Christ said, "This Gospel of the Kingdom shall be preached in all the world for a witness to all nations; and then shall the end come" (Matthew 24:14). Until that great day arrives, Evangelism Explosion will equip believers in and through local churches worldwide to multiply.

I focus on four factors that in the next decade should push us well along toward completing the job Jesus committed to His followers. They are prayer, purpose, principles and people. I purposely cover them in that order.

Prayer

You've seen the words on wall plaques: PRAYER CHANGES THINGS. If you are reading this book, you likely believe it. Probably you have seen prayer change attitudes, circumstances, people. And believing prayer will also change our world!

We at Evangelism Explosion want to see that happen. In our booklet, *Partners in Praying*, we suggest that:

- Prayer was the secret of Christ's evangelistic success (Mark 1:14, 35)
- Prayer expands our vision (Acts 11:5)
- Prayer opens closed doors (Colossians 4:2, 3)
- Prayer unleashes divine power (Ephesians 3:14-16)
- Prayer gives boldness to our witness (Ephesians 6:18, 19)
- Prayer brings wisdom about what to say (James 1:5)
- Prayer produces fruitfulness (John 15:5, 7)
- Prayer causes growth in new believers (Philippians 1:4, 6)
- Prayer impacts the world (Psalm 2:8)

In answer to believing prayer, God has advanced the ministry of EE beyond our wildest dreams! He has raised up workers, provided funds, opened doors. He has granted us wisdom, given us creative ideas, changed lives and churches. He has made resistant people receptive, brought amazing growth and extended the EE ministry into every nation and territory!

As you move with us into the next decade, we want you to join us in faithful, fervent prayer. We want you to have a share in the unfolding drama of what God is doing among the nations. For that to happen, your prayers and our prayers must be marked by . . .

Purpose

EE International is intensely concerned about where it is going and how it will get there. Not long ago I posed that very question to Founder and President, Dr. D. James Kennedy. "Now that EE has been planted in every nation and territory," I asked, "What is next?" Jim Kennedy's reply was immediate.

"Tom, we have 'lengthened the cords' of our ministry worldwide," he answered, alluding to Isaiah's prophecy (54:2). "Now let's 'strengthen the stakes' here in the U.S. and in all of those nations."

Shortly after that conversation, I met with our leadership team. Together we prayerfully discussed how we could "strengthen the stakes" that anchored the "lengthened ropes."

First, we refined EE's purpose statement:

The purpose of Evangelism Explosion International is to glorify God by equipping believers in and through local churches worldwide to multiply.

Next, we crafted a clear, concise statement of our vision:

Every nation equipping every people group and every age group to witness to every person.

Then we established objectives in ten vital areas. We called them "EE's Ten Vital Signs." When you see the doctor, he likely checks your vital signs: weight, temperature, blood pressure, heart beat, and lungs to determine your health. In the same way, we in EE have agreed upon ten vital signs to measure the "health" of our ministry in each nation. Our ten objectives are these:

- To assure top quality EE teachers, trainers, and witnesses worldwide
- To establish an effective EE ministry in local churches worldwide
- To provide top quality EE clinics and follow-through worldwide
- To supply top quality EE basic core materials in every principal language
- To train and appoint full-time leaders in every nation and territory
- To situate quality church-based clinics in every nation and territory
- To make covenants with EE leadership in every nation or territory
- To initiate EE for all age categories in every nation and territory
- To help national ministries establish EE in every people group
- To win to Christ and disciple the maximum number of people

Principles

Recently, at a dinner for clinic teachers, Dr. Kennedy was asked to explain what he did to get EE started so well. Here is his reply:

"First," Jim Kennedy said, "let me remind you that Thomas Edison, while inventing the incandescent light bulb, tried close to a thousand different things that failed before he discovered

The Next Ahead

the thing that, at last, produced the first light bulb.

"I must confess to you," Jim continued, "that as a young pastor with a passion to evangelize Fort Lauderdale, I tried at least 100 different things that didn't work before EE finally jelled into the ministry it is today. It is a ministry that last year alone trained tens of thousands of pastors and lay people worldwide. It is a ministry that saw more than 2,000,000 professions of faith in Christ in all 212 nations.

"In the forty-some years I have served God in Fort Lauderdale, I have launched and led nine ministries: Coral Ridge Presbyterian Church, Evangelism Explosion International, Westminster Academy, the local WAFG Christian radio station, the Truths that Transform radio hour, the internationally televised Coral Ridge Hour, Knox Theological Seminary, Reclaiming America, and The Center for Christian Statesmanship in Washington, D.C.

"But when all is said and done, and my life is finished" (and here Dr. Kennedy was very emphatic), "I believe the most significant thing God will have done through me will be Evangelism Explosion!"

Two or three weeks later, with that very powerful statement still in my mind, I invited Jim to lunch. Over the meal, I asked him to list for me some of the things that, in his mind, made EE "work" so successfully. Jim named 11 basic principles that emerged from his years of trial, error, and success. They are basic biblical principles applicable to every culture on every continent.

As I thought back over the development and worldwide expansion of EE, related in the preceding ten chapters, I saw these 11 principles stated and illustrated over and over. And as I think forward to the decade of ministry ahead, I consider it important—indeed, crucial—to restate clearly, succinctly, those

11 controlling principles:

1. EE is Bible-based and God-dependent. It stresses the importance of the witness's consistent lifestyle while enlisting the faithful intercession of dedicated prayer partners.

2. EE is mandated. From Christ's first and last commands, from His modeling of a faithful witness to the example of the early church, it is obvious that every believer is to witness both by his or her life and lips.

3. EE trains pastors. Pastors are trained in Leadership Training Clinics. They then return to their churches to model personal evangelism and equip members of their congregations to witness, and train others to witness.

4. EE emphasizes on-the-job training. Classroom teaching followed by on-the-job training dispels the witness's crippling fear and demonstrates that EE really works! "Evangelism is better caught than taught!"

5. EE diagnoses the other person's spiritual status. The two diagnostic questions deal with a person's universal concern about death. The answers reveal the person's true spiritual condition.

6. EE in incremental. The trainee learns the Gospel presentation bit-by-bit and step-by-step over an extended period of time (usually 13 to 16 weeks). During that time, the trainee continues to grow in his or her understanding of the Gospel and ability to witness.

7. EE has a memorized presentation. The basic outline, complete with Scriptures and illustrations, provides the witness with a tool for presenting the Gospel to non-Christians and for training fellow believers to do the same.

8. EE is relational. Whether in a first-time presentation of the Gospel or in a person's everyday network of relationships, friendship is emphasized as a crucial element in personal evangelism and discipleship.

9. EE is interdenominational. EE is not a para-church ministry, but is local-church-based and local-church-led. It ministers to and through churches of 400 denominations that subscribe to EE's evangelical statement of faith.

10. EE is indigenized. Although adhering to non-negotiable, controlling principles, EE adapts to the culture of every nation, territory and people group with the ultimate goal of making each ministry self-supporting, self-managed and self-propagating.

11. EE multiplies. Teacher/trainers, through a certification process, equip witnesses who, in turn, become trainers of others to win people to Christ. Thus, they continue to reproduce themselves.

One day, Jim Kennedy and I will have passed off the scene. We pray that the leaders God raises up in our stead will hold firmly to these principles. Until Jesus Christ returns, may EE apply them diligently in America and in every other nation, territory, and people group of the world.

People

Carl Sandburg in his poem, "I Am the People, the Mob," from his book *Complete Poems*, uttered a profound thought when he asked, "Do you know that all the great work of the world is done through people?"

Without question, EE's most valuable resource is its people. Pastors. Missionaries. Teachers. Laity. Men. Women. Youth. Kids. Seniors. To write about the development of EE and the future of EE without focusing on the people of EE would be impossible. The history of EE is the story of God working in and through people. You have met a number of the choice people in the pages of this book. But let me tell you of several lesser-known people whom God has used profoundly in the ministry of EE.

The Other Billy Graham

The first is a pastor by the name of Billy Graham. No, not the renowned evangelist, but the Pastor of Evangelism at North Mobile Baptist Church, Mobile, Alabama. Billy invited me to speak at his church's enlistment banquet and again on Sunday morning. He and an EE volunteer met me at the airport and took me to Billy's home, where I would stay for the weekend.

On the way to the banquet I learned that Billy had been born blind and with Muscular Dystrophy. Life expectancy: eight years, all of it confined to a wheelchair. Obviously, he had outlasted the eight years, but he was still in a wheelchair. Billy's wife, his only eyes and feet, had died in year 13 of their marriage.

Complaints? None! Billy exuded joy, love, and praise. As we waited for the banquet to begin, I noticed that everyone hugged

Billy. It was evident that they loved him dearly. And why not? After all, he had taught EE to most of them and trained them in its use.

To get the ministry started he had taken teams out five nights a week. I asked someone how he managed to get around for on-the-job training.

"Oh, his team members drive and help him up to the doors in his wheel chair," one of the trainers explained. "But when we visit apartments on the second floor, Billy climbs the stairs on his hands and knees." No one ever turned Billy's teams away when they saw the effort he went through to visit them!

The banquet was awesome. People were excited about joining such a dynamic ministry. Billy is a clinic teacher and now hosts EE clinics at his church in Mobile.

Anne Kennedy

You met Mrs. Anne Kennedy earlier in the book, the long-time partner of EE's founder. My wife, Donna, and I visited with Anne at her home not long ago. I asked Anne, "In the early years of your ministry with Jim, what did you think about Jim's desire to win people to Christ?"

"Well," she responded, "after he became a Christian and before we were married, it was so important for Jim to share his faith that he promised the Lord he would not go to bed until he had shared the Gospel with at least one person. He impressed on me the importance of sharing our faith. So we did that even before we were married."

I probed some more. "Is it true, Anne, that sometimes in your ministry you kept a little tape recorder in your purse? When you met people at the Visitor's Fellowship, you would ask them to spell out their name to make sure you got it right?"

"I still do that every Sunday," Anne replied. "Then, on Monday I go to the office or call the office and get the address, call the visitor, and make an appointment. At first, I went with Jim. But now that I am a trainer, I take my team with me.

"Back when we were still meeting at McNab Elementary School, I met a young woman named Beverly Abell at some kind of a brunch we were both attending. After some conversation, I asked her if Jim and I could visit her and her husband, Wally. They both made professions of faith. Later Bev became a well-known Bible teacher. I have seen magazine articles by her. She has really been making a difference for Christ.

"On another occasion, I called on a woman from Coral Springs who professed Christ on December 6, 1995. Scarcely four months later, she was walking in her neighborhood when teens shot and killed her. Sharing the Gospel of Christ with her was certainly a divine appointment."

Anne explained how she remembered names and details so well. "The particulars of every call I make I enter into a little book. I also include the person's address and phone number. If it is a family and they have children, I enter the children's names. Some who were not ready to make a decision for Christ when we first met, tell me seven or eight years later, 'I really understand now what you were trying to tell me so long ago.' I have all of them listed in my book. I could not live without that book! I can't imagine calling on people and never knowing what has happened to them!"

I had still another question for this gracious woman. "You are sometimes asked why a pastor's wife should be in EE. What do you say?"

"Well, first I say that winning people to Christ is a Bible command. EE is a systematic way to obey it. We ministers' wives should be examples. Besides that, it's a way I can meet people who come to our church and visit them in their homes. Also, my prayer partners and my trainees over the years have all become very special friends."

"What about Jennifer, your daughter?" I asked. "Did she feel deprived?"

"Jim and I had been married six years when Jennifer came along. I just had to get a lot of baby sitters! Jennifer never seemed to resent our being gone. When Jennifer was in fourth grade at Westminster Academy, Winnie Wilkinson trained the whole class in EE. Later, when she moved back from college, she started right in again with EE. Jennifer has been in EE every semester for eighteen years.

"Tom, I really see EE as my reason for living. Winning people to Christ is the one thing we do that has eternal consequences. Knowing how to witness is the most important thing I have ever learned."

Ruth Clark

The third person is an EE trainer, Mrs. Ruth Clark. The year after Donna and I moved to Fort Lauderdale, John and Ruth Clark invited us for dinner. I asked them what they thought of EE. John began: "Ruth told me she wasn't ready for Heaven. I reminded her that she had trusted Christ as her Savior, she had worked hard in the church and had lived a good life." Then Ruth joined in, "I told John I wasn't ready for Heaven because I was going alone, not taking one person with me that I had led to Christ. To make matters worse, my 15-year-old grandson, David, came here from Memphis, Tennessee, and asked me, 'Grandma, what do I need to do to go to Heaven?' I didn't know how to lead him to Christ and he went back to Tennessee, leaving me a very sad grandma.

"Finally, I said to John, 'That EE course is pretty tough, but I'm going to sign up next semester!'"

John interrupted. "You should have seen our home, Tom, while she was taking that course! You would've thought it was an advertising agency. She had different parts of the EE outline pasted all over the walls. A verse of Scripture over the bathroom sink. Illustrations pasted here and there. Ruth was determined she was going to learn the presentation, and this was her way to review her memory work all day long."

"I passed the course," Ruth added, "got my certificate and pin and flew up to Memphis to find my grandson. 'David,' I asked, 'Do you still want to know how to get to Heaven?' He did, and I had the thrill of leading him to Christ. Then he took me to see his friends, and I led many of his friends to Christ."

"My childhood girl friend also gave her heart to Christ," John added. "So Ruth came back to Ft. Lauderdale and is now serving as a trainer in her third semester of EE!"

As I became involved in the Ft. Lauderdale EE training, I noticed that John and Ruth were there every week. In fact, Ruth became one of the favorite trainers. During the EE clinics, Ruth would take out experienced pastors for their on-the-job training.

One clinic evening, as the trainers reported their successes, Ruth admitted sadly that her team hadn't had a very productive evening. While the other teams were reporting, Ruth slipped out into the foyer and, before the report session was over, reappeared with a policeman on her arm.

"Officer," Ruth said, "tell these fine people what you just did."

"Well," the police officer explained with some hesitance, "I pulled into your parking lot and asked this nice lady why there were so many cars here tonight, and she gave to me the gift of eternal life!"

As I write this, Ruth, at age 75, is not well. She may not have many more days with us. But one thing I know for certain. Ruth is ready for heaven, and she's going to be taking a whole lot of people with her! Moreover, she has trained many pastors and lay people to continue the ministry so dear to her heart.

Robert Strickland

Robert Strickland is an EE trainee from Freehold, New Jersey. At age 89, Robert attended a Reclaiming America For Christ conference here in Fort Lauderdale and heard Rev. John Sorensen, our Vice President for Ministry Advancement, introduce EE. Having some unsaved neighbors he wanted to win to Christ, Robert asked, "John, can a man up in years like I am still win somebody to Christ?"

"Robert," John replied, "go home and recruit your pastor to go to an EE clinic; then ask him to come back and train you. I guarantee you that a year from now you will have led at least one person to Christ!" Robert wasn't successful in recruiting his pastor to attend a clinic, but he did find a church 20 miles from his home that used EE. Every Tuesday evening he drove there for EE training.

A year later, at age 90, Robert attended another Reclaiming America conference. As John tells it, "This year Robert didn't hobble down to see me. He literally ran down the aisle, calling out to me.

"'Robert,' I asked, 'did you win one person to Christ this past year?' Robert looked rather serious and replied, 'No!' Then he held up five fingers and said gleefully, 'Praise God, John. I led *five* to Christ! Two church visitors and the three neighbors

I have prayed for, for so long!'"

Dolly and Fred Stephens

Dolly and Fred Stephens started taking EE at Coral Ridge Presbyterian Church in 1976. When Dolly retired, she wondered what she would do with herself. Then she decided to come over to EE headquarters, just two blocks from her home, to help in the clinics and wherever else she could be used.

Every Monday, Tuesday, and Wednesday, since late 1992, Dolly has entered data into computers, answered telephones, stuffed and mailed letters, and cared for anything else that could use her attention. Whenever we have out-of-town EE visitors needing a place to stay, Fred and Dolly open their guest room for as long as our visitors stay.

"After all," Dolly says, "we're near the office and church. It's quite convenient for them."

Fred and Dolly love EE so much that they have helped pastors in five different churches launch an EE ministry. After about three years, the EE ministry in one church has stabilized, and Fred and Dolly move on to help another pastor and his congregation. Right now they're serving on Monday evenings with Pastor Stephen Geiger at Northeast Baptist Church in Fort Lauderdale.

Volunteers like Fred and Dolly are the backbone of the EE ministry around the world. Committed EE pastors like Billy and pastors' wives like Anne are equipping their saints in churches on every continent.

Increasingly, dedicated trainers like Ruth are being used of God to win people to Christ and to train others to win people to Christ. More and more hardworking, faithful trainees like Robert are leading their neighbors to Christ through EE. *But they're still too few in number.* EE needs many more "Billies," more "Annes," more "Ruths," more "Roberts," more "Fred and Dollys"! As you are reading this chapter now, will you commit yourself to be one of those whom God uses in this exciting ministry? You you can change the world for Jesus Christ.

How?

If you are a pastor or pastor's wife, write or call to register for one of the upcoming EE Leadership Training Clinics. If you are a lay person, talk to your pastor about launching EE in your church. If your church already has EE, see what you can do as a volunteer to accelerate and strengthen the EE training.

If you are a missionary and want to serve more directly with EE, see if your mission might second you to Evangelism Explosion International. EE has openings in North America and in many other world areas.

If you are retired and have adequate support to serve full or part-time with EE, let us know. The possibilities with EE are limitless. The opportunities are mind-boggling. The rewards are out of this world!

Would you like to be a world-changer? EE has come a long way in the 40 years since Jim Kennedy challenged his small congregation with the words, "We can change the world!" The past years of EE's growth and expansion have been dramatic, but the future promises to be infinitely more exciting! Together, let's believe that God, by His powerful Gospel, for His greater glory, and through His equipped Church, *will indeed* change the world!

*Evangelism Explosion International Board and Vice Presidents
March 2000*

Appendix

Back through the Years in Photos

Rev. Archie Parrish, EE's first Executive Vice President

Dr. Woody Lajara, EE's 3rd Executive Vice President

Rev. T.M. Moore, EE's 2nd Executive Vice President visiting with Jerry and Ande Stapella.

Merlin (Mike) Feather, EE's 4th Executive Vice President

Dr. Tom Stebbins, EE's 5th and present Executive Vice President addressing EE Clinic Teachers Advance

Rev. Buddy Gaines, International Vice President, with Dr. and Mrs. Nickolay Revtov, Dir. of EE Eurasia

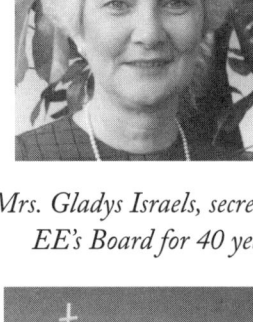

Mrs. Gladys Israels, secretary of EE's Board for 40 years

EE youth mission trip to Africa

EE International Headquarters in Fort Lauderdale, Florida

Back through the Years in Pictures

Rev. Vic Jakopson, EE's 1st Vice President of Europe

Rev. Wade Weaver (right), EE's 2nd Vice President for Europe visiting Bosnia

Rev. Jack Hawthorne, EE's 1st Director for the Caribbean

Rev. Tim McGlame, EE's 2nd Director for the Caribbean

Asian leaders join Dr. and Mrs Kennedy for 25th Anniversary

Explosion of Evangelism

Rev. David Clippard, EE Vice President for North America 1984-1988, visiting with Martie Gaines

Rev. Tommy Hinson, EE Vice President for North America from 1988-1995

Rev. Shelby Smith, EE Vice President for North America from 1997-2000

Rev. John Sorensen, EE Vice President for Ministry Advancement

Charlie Hainline and Carrie Davies, sharing EE presentation

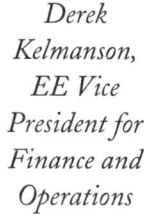

Derek Kelmanson, EE Vice President for Finance and Operations